MATHS ON TARGET

Year 6

Stephen Pearce

Elmwood Press

First published 2008 by
Elmwood Press
80 Attimore Road
Welwyn Garden City
Herts. AL8 6LP
Tel. 01707 333232

Reprinted in 2009

ISBN 9781 902 214 948

Numerical answers are published in a separate book.

Typeset and illustrated by Tech-Set Ltd., Gateshead, Tyne and Wear.
Printed and bound in Spain on behalf of JFDi Print Services Ltd.

PREFACE

Maths on Target has been written for pupils in Year 6 and their teachers.

The intention of the book is to provide teachers with material to teach all the objectives as set out in the yearly programme in the renewed Primary Framework for Mathematics.

The structure of **Maths on Target** matches that of the renewed framework. It is arranged in five blocks, A–E, each of which consists of three units. To ensure progression throughout the year the units are best taught in the order in which they appear in both this book and the exemplar planning structure for Year 6 in the renewed framework.

	Block A	Block B	Block C	Block D	Block E
Term 1	Unit 1	Unit 1	Unit 1	Unit 1	Unit 1
Term 2	Unit 2	Unit 2	Unit 2	Unit 2	Unit 2
Term 3	Unit 3	Unit 3	Unit 3	Unit 3	Unit 3

Each unit in **Maths on Target** consists of lessons based upon the learning overview for that unit in the renewed framework. Each lesson is divided into four sections:

Introduction: the learning intention expressed as an 'I can' statement and, where necessary, clearly worked examples.

Section A: activities based upon work previously covered. This generally matches the objectives for Year 5 pupils. This section can be used to remind children of work previously covered, as well as providing material for the less confident child.

Section B: activities based upon the objectives for Year 6 pupils. Most children should be able to work successfully at this level.

Section C: activities providing extension material for the faster workers and for those who need to be moved quickly onto more challenging tasks. Problems in Section C can also provide useful material for discussion in the plenary session.

The correspondence of the three sections A–C to the objectives for different year groups provides a simple, manageable structure for planning differentiated activities and for both the formal and informal assessment of children's progress. The commonality of the content pitched at different levels also allows for progression within the lesson. Children acquiring confidence at one level find they can successfully complete activities at the next level.

The author is indebted to many colleagues who have assisted him in this work. He is particularly grateful to Sharon Granville and Debra Turner for their invaluable advice and assistance.

Stephen Pearce

CONTENTS

I can find the rule for a number sequence.

To find the rule that links the numbers study the gaps.

Examples

4	0	−4	−8	−12	The rule is *subtract 4*.
3	6	12	24	48	The rule is *multiply by 2*.
1	3	6	10	15	The rule is *add one more each time*.

A

Write the first six numbers in each sequence.

	Start at	Rule		Start at	Rule		Start at	Rule
1	210	−4	6	0·6	+0·1	11	0·01	+0·02
2	65	+4	7	201	+101	12	3·5	−0·5
3	$\frac{1}{2}$	$+\frac{1}{4}$	8	2	×2	13	5	$-\frac{1}{2}$
4	−60	+5	9	425	−50	14	1·25	+0·25
5	−1	−1	10	−3	−2	15	−18	−2

B

Complete these sequences by filling in the boxes. Write the rule each time.

1. −4 −3 −2 −1 ☐ ☐ ☐
2. 1·2 2·4 3·6 4·8 ☐ ☐ ☐
3. ☐ ☐ ☐ 2 $1\frac{2}{3}$ $1\frac{1}{3}$ 1
4. ☐ ☐ ☐ 230 330 430 530
5. 19 38 ☐ ☐ 114 133
6. 0·09 0·18 ☐ ☐ ☐ 0·54 0·63
7. −33 −23 −13 −3 ☐ ☐ ☐
8. $\frac{2}{9}$ $\frac{4}{9}$ ☐ ☐ ☐ $1\frac{3}{9}$ $1\frac{5}{9}$

9. 1 4 9 ☐ 25 ☐ ☐
10. 100 ☐ 81 ☐ 66 ☐ 55
11. ☐ −5 ☐ ☐ 4 7 10
12. ☐ 4 ☐ ☐ −5 −10 −16
13. ☐ ☐ ☐ −5 −8 −11 −14
14. 2 4 ☐ 16 ☐ 64 ☐
15. 290 ☐ 170 ☐ ☐ 65 50
16. 1·3 ☐ 2·1 ☐ ☐ 3·3 3·7

C

Copy the sequences and write the next three numbers. Write down the rule each time.

1. −8 −6 −4 −2
2. 2·1 4·2 6·3 8·4
3. 25 20 15 10
4. 1 $2\frac{1}{5}$ $3\frac{2}{5}$ $4\frac{3}{5}$
5. −15 −11 −7 −3
6. 10·0 10·1 10·3 10·6
7. 1 3 9 27
8. 15 11 7 3
9. $\frac{3}{5}$ $1\frac{1}{5}$ $1\frac{4}{5}$ $2\frac{2}{5}$
10. 49 64 81 100
11. 2 3 5 9 17
12. 0·05 0·1 0·15 0·2
13. 1·0 0·75 0·5 0·25
14. $\frac{1}{10}$ $\frac{2}{10}$ $\frac{4}{10}$ $\frac{8}{10}$
15. 3·0 2·25 1·5 0·75
16. −21 −15 −10 −6
17. 2 6 12 20
18. 0·3 0·41 0·53 0·66

I can estimate numbers on a number line.

A

Estimate the numbers shown by the arrows.

1
100   200

2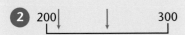
200   300

3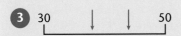
30   50

4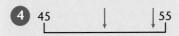
45   55

5 0   25

6 This bar line graph shows the percentage mark achieved by children in a test.

Allan
Brett
Colin
Dylan
Eddie
Frank

Allan got 100%.

a) Who got 50%?

b) Who got twice as many as Colin?

c) Who got half as many as Brett?

d) Estimate the mark achieved by each of the five boys.

B

Estimate the numbers shown by the arrows.

1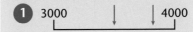
3000   4000

2 0   10000

3 −5   0

4 0   1

5 −25   0

6 Six friends ordered pizzas. When they had finished eating, their pizzas looked like this:

Estelle   Wendy   Jenny

Gill   Judy   Sharon

Who had eaten:

a) twice as much as Gill?

b) five times as much as Judy?

c) half as much as Sharon?

7 Estimate the proportion of each pizza which had been eaten. Give your answer as a percentage.

C

Estimate the numbers shown by the arrows.

1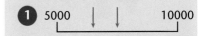
5000   10000

2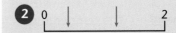
0   2

3 −20   0

4 5   7.5

5 −50   0

6 Estimate the number of words in your reading book. Explain your method.

Use your method to estimate the number of words in:

a) a picture book

b) a dictionary

c) an encyclopaedia.

7 Estimate the number of times someone blinks in a day. Explain your method.

I can order negative numbers and find the difference between a pair of negative numbers and between a negative number and a positive number.

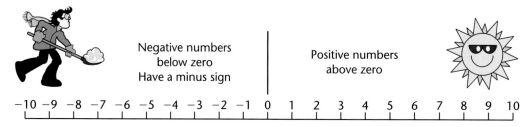

Negative numbers
below zero
Have a minus sign

Positive numbers
above zero

−10 −9 −8 −7 −6 −5 −4 −3 −2 −1   0   1   2   3   4   5   6   7   8   9   10

Example   The temperature is 6°C. It falls 8°C.
What is the new temperature?   Answer −2°C.

A

Copy and complete by writing the missing numbers in the boxes

1 −7 ☐ ☐ ☐ 1 3 5

2 10 7 4 1 ☐ ☐ ☐

3 −13 −10 −7 ☐ ☐ ☐ 5

4 −10 −6 ☐ ☐ ☐ 10 14

5 6 4 ☐ ☐ ☐ −4 −6

6 ☐ ☐ ☐ −1 −3 −5 −7

7 9 6 3 0 ☐ ☐ ☐

8 11 7 3 ☐ ☐ ☐ −13

Put these numbers in order, smallest first.

9

−8   0
6   −5
−3   4

10
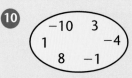
−10   3
1   −4
8   −1

11
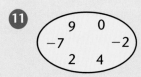
9   0
−7   −2
2   4

12
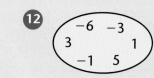
−6   −3
3   1
−1   5

13 What temperatures are shown by the letters on the scale?

14 Which letter shows the coldest temperature?

15 Give the difference in temperature between:

   a) A and B   **b)** A and C   **c)** B and C.

16 What would the temperature be:

   a) if it was at A and fell 13°C?

   b) if it was at B and rose 19°C?

   c) if it was at C and fell 15°C?

17 The temperature is −5°C and it rises by 10°C.
What is the new temperature?

18 The temperature is 3°C and it falls by 10°C.
What is the new temperature?

B

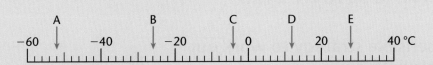

A   B   C   D   E

−60   −40   −20   0   20   40 °C

1 What temperatures are shown by the letters?

2 Give the difference in temperature between:

a) C and D   **c)** C and E

b) B and C   **d)** B and D

3 What would the temperature be if it was:

a) at A and rose 24°C?   **c)** at C and fell 36°C?

b) at D and fell 18°C?   **d)** at B and rose 36°C?

Copy and complete the tables showing changes in temperature.

4

OLD	CHANGE	NEW
5°C	−9°C	−4°C
−3°C	+10°C	
−19°C	+13°C	
9°C	−15°C	
−12°C	+8°C	
13°C	−16°C	

5

OLD	CHANGE	NEW
−6°C	+8°C	2°C
	−6°C	−2°C
	+4°C	−13°C
	−8°C	−4°C
	+20°C	12°C
	−12°C	−17°C

6

OLD	CHANGE	NEW
9°C		−4°C
1°C		−11°C
4°C		−5°C
−5°C		9°C
−3°C		−16°C
6°C		−4°C

C

Copy and complete the table showing the average temperatures recorded in January and July at places in different countries in the Northern Hemisphere.

1

Country	January	July	Range
U.S.A.	−7°C	26°C	33°C
Greenland	−35°C	−1°C	
Germany	−2°C	18°C	
Japan	−9°C	21°C	
Switzerland	−6°C	11°C	
Iran	−3°C		40°C
China	−19°C		42°C
Poland	−5°C		20°C
Norway	−14°C		23°C
Korea	−22°C		42°C
Romania		24°C	29°C
Russia		18°C	58°C
Canada		20°C	39°C
Sweden		16°C	20°C

2 The highest temperature ever recorded on Earth is 56°C. The lowest is −70°C. What is the range of temperature recorded on Earth?

3 The range of temperature on Mars is 174°C. The highest temperature reached is 37°C. What is the lowest?

4 The range of temperature on Mercury is 600°C. The lowest temperature reached is −173°C. What is the highest?

I choose a sensible strategy to work out a mental calculation.

Examples

ADDITION AND SUBTRACTION

Partitioning
328 + 63
320 + 60 + 8 + 3
380 + 11
391

Using Nearest Whole Number And Adjusting
4·5 + 3·9
4·5 + 4·0 − 0·1
8·5 − 0·1
8·4

546 − 75
546 − 70 − 5
476 − 5
471

Counting Up
7003 − 3995

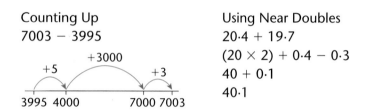

5 + 3000 + 3 = 3008

Using Near Doubles
20·4 + 19·7
(20 × 2) + 0·4 − 0·3
40 + 0·1
40·1

MULTIPLICATION AND DIVISION

Using Factors
252 ÷ 18
252 ÷ 2 ÷ 3 ÷ 3
126 ÷ 3 ÷ 3
42 ÷ 3
14

Partitioning
5·3 × 6
(5 × 6) + (0·3 × 6)
30 + 1·8
31·8

Multiply By 19/21 etc.
17 × 51
(17 × 50) + (17 × 1)
850 + 17
867

Using Doubling And Halving
14 × 15
14 × 10 = 140
140 ÷ 2 = 70
14 × 15 = 210

A

Choose one method for each group of six problems.

1 8 × 21
2 14 × 19
3 18 × 21
4 12 × 19
5 24 × 21
6 17 × 19

25 46 + 53
26 57 + 61
27 79 + 84
28 2·2 + 2·4
29 4·5 + 4·4
30 4·1 + 3·8

7 1·5 + 0·9
8 6·2 − 0·9
9 7·1 + 1·1
10 3·9 − 1·1
11 4·8 + 0·9
12 2·6 − 1·1

31 16 × 50
32 37 × 50
33 8 × 15
34 12 × 15
35 28 × 5
36 34 × 5

13 604 − 396
14 908 − 569
15 803 − 285
16 6000 − 2994
17 5000 − 1976
18 6007 − 3995

37 26 × 4
38 49 × 5
39 38 × 6
40 27 × 7
41 44 × 8
42 26 × 9

19 14 × 6
20 15 × 8
21 17 × 9
22 156 ÷ 12
23 180 ÷ 15
24 210 ÷ 14

43 242 + 53
44 148 + 25
45 317 + 34
46 493 − 76
47 216 − 53
48 524 − 37

B

Choose one method for each group of six problems.

1. $7.3 - 1.9$
2. $3.7 + 2.9$
3. $8.3 - 4.1$
4. $6.8 + 2.1$
5. $5.5 - 2.9$
6. $3.7 + 4.1$

7. 72×6
8. 73×7
9. 84×8
10. 6.9×7
11. 8.6×9
12. 5.7×8

13. $6800 + 2500$
14. $0.5 + 0.28$
15. $0.65 + 0.37$
16. $0.6 - 0.17$
17. $8100 - 2900$
18. $0.84 - 0.35$

19. 16×51
20. 12×49
21. 23×51
22. 14×99
23. 17×101
24. 22×99

25. 26×15
26. 33×15
27. 29×25
28. 35×25
29. 18×28
30. 16×19

31. $801 - 587$
32. $726 - 169$
33. $635 - 272$
34. $6000 - 3655$
35. $9008 - 4963$
36. $8016 - 2979$

37. 45×18
38. 17×27
39. 19×14
40. $320 \div 16$
41. $336 \div 24$
42. $273 \div 21$

43. $302 + 294$
44. $413 + 391$
45. $387 + 415$
46. $2.7 + 2.8$
47. $4.9 + 4.8$
48. $6.2 + 5.9$

C

Choose one method for each group of six problems.

1. $8100 - \square = 2776$
2. $7200 - \square = 3892$
3. $6300 - \square = 3765$
4. $9100 - \square = 4688$
5. $7300 - \square = 3764$
6. $8200 - \square = 2687$

7. $\square + 4700 = 9600$
8. $\square + 5.8 = 11.24$
9. $\square + 0.64 = 1.52$
10. $\square - 3600 = 6800$
11. $\square - 7.5 = 24.61$
12. $\square - 0.48 = 0.54$

13. 3.1×18
14. 2.3×14
15. 1.7×15
16. 15×6.3
17. 25×3.9
18. 24×4.5

19. $\square \div 7 = 8.3$
20. $\square \div 8 = 9.7$
21. $\square \div 9 = 6.9$
22. $\square \div 6 = 0.46$
23. $\square \div 8 = 0.84$
24. $\square \div 7 = 0.67$

25. 12×3.6
26. 16×4.5
27. 14×1.8
28. $36.8 \div 16$
29. $48.3 \div 21$
30. $3.96 \div 18$

31. $\square - 19.6 = 20.7$
32. $\square - 50.8 = 49.5$
33. $\square - 25.6 = 24.8$
34. $\square - 31.4 = 29.3$
35. $\square - 18.7 = 21.6$
36. $\square - 41.2 = 39.9$

37. $\square \div 41 = 16$
38. $\square \div 59 = 12$
39. $\square \div 39 = 13$
40. $\square \div 61 = 14$
41. $\square \div 59 = 17$
42. $\square \div 41 = 18$

43. $\square + 4.9 = 8.8$
44. $\square + 6.2 = 12.3$
45. $\square + 4.7 = 9.7$
46. $\square - 4.1 = 7.6$
47. $\square - 5.8 = 2.5$
48. $\square - 5.2 = 13.4$

I can round large numbers to the nearest multiple of 10, 100 or 1000 and decimals to the nearest whole number or tenth.

Examples

Rounding to the nearest 10	329 → 330	1264 → 1260
Rounding to the nearest 100	638 → 600	2351 → 2400
Rounding to the nearest 1000	4835 → 5000	13 294 → 13 000
Rounding to the nearest 1	19·7 → 20	4·28 → 4

A

Round to the nearest:

 10   1000

1 288
2 641
3 67
4 365
5 3799

11 4630
12 7373
13 12 517
14 5995
15 26 478

 100   1

6 743
7 3450
8 1365
9 216
10 4194

16 11·4
17 5·9
18 78·2
19 19·81
20 3·54

Approximate by rounding to the nearest 10.

21 148 + 73
22 542 + 267
23 638 − 94
24 762 − 357

25 68 × 5
26 79 × 9
27 158 ÷ 4
28 317 ÷ 8

B

Round these football crowds:

a) to the nearest 1000
b) to the nearest 100.

1 Arsenal   60 051
2 Chelsea   37 646
3 Leeds   39 837
4 Liverpool   44 718
5 Man. Utd.   75 581
6 Newcastle   50 078

Round these distances to:

a) the nearest metre
b) the nearest 10 cm.

7 3·27 m
8 9·34 m
9 8·58 m
10 11·93 m

11 6·05 m
12 2·89 m
13 27·46 m
14 15·62 m

Approximate by rounding to the nearest whole one.

15 18·2 + 6·7
16 20·8 − 4·19
17 6·9 × 3·1
18 14·6 × 5·2
19 12·4 ÷ 2·1
20 41·6 ÷ 6·9

C

Would you round the following to the nearest 10, 100, 1000, 10 000, 100 000 or million?

1 pages in a set of encyclopaedias
2 people in the UK
3 children in your school
4 the distance to Rome in metres
5 days you have lived
6 people on a full bus
7 words in the Bible
8 children in a Secondary School
9 the capacity of a bath in millilitres
10 an adult's weight in grams
11 the length of the Thames in miles
12 miles to Australia
13 Make some of these estimates. Explain your method each time.

I can multiply decimal numbers by one-digit whole numbers.

Examples

```
   24·3          or      24·3              2·43        or       2·43
 ×    6                ×    6            ×    6               ×    6
  120·0    20 × 6      145·8             12·00    2 × 6        14·58
   24·0     4 × 6       2 1               2·40    0·4 × 6       2 1
    1·8    0·3 × 6                         0·18    0·03 × 6
  145·8                                  14·58
```

A

Copy and complete.

1   8·6
    ×   2

        8·0 × 2
        0·6 × 2
        ___

2   3·4
    ×   8

        3·0 × 8
        0·4 × 8
        ___

3   2·3
    ×   6

        2·0 × 6
        0·3 × 6
        ___

4   6·9
    ×   5

        6·0 × 5
        0·9 × 5
        ___

Work out

5 3·5 × 9   **9** 5·4 × 6

6 4·2 × 7   **10** 7·5 × 8

7 2·8 × 4   **11** 6·3 × 7

8 9·7 × 3   **12** 4·6 × 9

B

Copy and complete.

1   49·3   **5**   5·34
    ×   3   ×   9

2   32·4   **6**   8·97
    ×   6   ×   5

3   74·2   **7**   9·46
    ×   8   ×   4

4   61·5   **8**   3·85
    ×   7   ×   8

Work out

9 24·8 × 7   **13** 0·47 × 9

10 95·3 × 8   **14** 8·27 × 8

11 37·8 × 4   **15** 9·73 × 3

12 65·4 × 6   **16** 3·95 × 7

17 A hose uses 5·82 litres of water in one minute. How much water does it use in 4 minutes?

18 One stone equals 6·35 kg. Niamh weighs 8 stones. How much does she weigh in kilograms?

C

Work out

1 31·63 × 6

2 12·47 × 5

3 59·38 × 3

4 57·23 × 9

5 83·62 × 7

6 46·71 × 8

7 2·945 × 4

8 7·283 × 9

9 4·874 × 7

10 9·248 × 8

11 6·751 × 6

12 7·635 × 9

13 A plane flies at an average speed of 19·76 km per minute. How far does it fly in one hour?

I can divide decimal numbers by one-digit whole numbers.

Examples

218 ÷ 4

Estimate first
4 × 50 = 200
4 × 60 = 240
200 < 218 < 240
50 < Answer < 60

```
      218
  −   200  (4 × 50)
       18
  −    16  (4 × 4)
        2
```
Answer 54 r2

21·6 ÷ 4

Estimate first
4 × 5·0 = 20·0
4 × 6·0 = 24·0
20·0 < 21·6 < 24·0
5·0 < Answer < 6·0

```
     21·6
  −  20·0  (4 × 5·0)
      1·6
  −   1·6  (4 × 0·4)
        0
```
Answer 5·4

67 ÷ 5

```
      67
  −   50   (5 × 10)
      17
  −   15   (5 × 3)
      2·0
  −   2·0  (5 × 0·4)
        0
```
Answer 13·4

A

Work out

1. 116 ÷ 5
2. 110 ÷ 6
3. 170 ÷ 7
4. 199 ÷ 8
5. 116 ÷ 9
6. 238 ÷ 5
7. 253 ÷ 8
8. 261 ÷ 7
9. 142 ÷ 6
10. 193 ÷ 9
11. 171 ÷ 4
12. 212 ÷ 8
13. 211 ÷ 6
14. 306 ÷ 7
15. 329 ÷ 5
16. 320 ÷ 9

B

Work out

1. 16·8 ÷ 2
2. 22·2 ÷ 6
3. 38·5 ÷ 5
4. 47·7 ÷ 9
5. 26·1 ÷ 3
6. 33·6 ÷ 7
7. 25·2 ÷ 4
8. 60·8 ÷ 8
9. 21·5 ÷ 5
10. 68·4 ÷ 9
11. 59·5 ÷ 7
12. 16·2 ÷ 3
13. 13·4 ÷ 2
14. 34·4 ÷ 8
15. 17·6 ÷ 4
16. 50·4 ÷ 6

17. An astronaut weighs 76·8 kilograms. On the Moon he weighs one sixth of his weight on Earth. How much does he weigh on the Moon?

C

Work out to one decimal place.

1. 83·0 ÷ 5
2. 26·0 ÷ 4
3. 67·0 ÷ 2
4. 19·0 ÷ 5
5. 42·0 ÷ 4
6. 51·0 ÷ 2
7. 94·0 ÷ 5
8. 78·0 ÷ 4
9. 89 ÷ 2
10. 127 ÷ 5
11. 294 ÷ 4
12. 115 ÷ 2
13. 366 ÷ 5
14. 70 ÷ 4
15. 33 ÷ 2
16. 260 ÷ 8

17. A rope is 8·4 m long. It is cut into five equal lengths. How long is each length?

18. A bag of potatoes weighs 12·5 kg. What is the weight of half the bag?

19. A car has a full petrol tank containing 37 litres. One quarter is used. How much petrol is left?

I can place brackets to make a calculation correct.

Examples

$4 + (3 \times 7) = 4 + 21 = 25$
$(4 + 3) \times 7 = 7 \times 7 = 49$

Using a calculator
$100 - (62 \cdot 8 \div 16) = 100 - 3 \cdot 925 = 96 \cdot 075$
$(100 - 62 \cdot 8) \div 16 = 37 \cdot 2 \div 16 = 2 \cdot 325$

A

Work out the brackets first.

1. $(3 + 6) \times 7$
2. $3 + (6 \times 7)$
3. $(12 - 8) \div 2$
4. $12 - (8 \div 2)$
5. $(30 \div 6) + 4$
6. $30 \div (6 + 4)$
7. $(9 \times 8) - 3$
8. $9 \times (8 - 3)$
9. $(40 \div 5) \times 4$
10. $40 \div (5 \times 4)$

Put the brackets in the right place to make the calculation correct.

11. $56 - 8 \times 2 = 96$
12. $27 \div 9 + 3 = 6$
13. $8 \times 4 - 2 = 30$
14. $6 + 5 \times 3 = 21$
15. $60 - 50 \div 5 = 50$
16. $20 \div 4 \times 4 = 20$
17. $6 \times 8 + 4 = 52$
18. $42 \div 8 - 1 = 6$
19. $26 - 9 + 3 = 14$
20. $80 \div 4 \div 2 = 40$

B

Use a calculator if needed.

1. $(15 \times 9) \div 3$
2. $15 \times (9 \div 3)$
3. $(9 \cdot 6 + 3 \cdot 2) \div 8$
4. $9 \cdot 6 + (3 \cdot 2 \div 8)$
5. $(5 \cdot 8 - 0 \cdot 6) \times 3$
6. $5 \cdot 8 - (0 \cdot 6 \times 3)$
7. $(272 \div 17) - 9$
8. $272 \div (17 - 9)$
9. $(3 \cdot 25 \times 8) + 12$
10. $3 \cdot 25 \times (8 + 12)$

Place the brackets to make the calculation correct.

11. $4 \cdot 8 - 1 \cdot 5 \div 3 = 1 \cdot 1$
12. $7 \cdot 2 \div 6 + 2 = 0 \cdot 9$
13. $0 \cdot 5 \times 8 - 1 \cdot 5 = 2 \cdot 5$
14. $19 + 16 \times 7 = 131$
15. $4 \cdot 7 - 1 \cdot 2 + 0 \cdot 9 = 2 \cdot 6$
16. $504 \div 14 \times 3 = 108$
17. $34 \times 8 \div 5 = 54 \cdot 4$
18. $9 \cdot 3 - 5 \cdot 9 \times 2 = 6 \cdot 8$
19. $12 \div 5 \div 4 = 9 \cdot 6$
20. $7 \times 4 \cdot 15 + 2 \cdot 3 = 45 \cdot 15$

C

Copy and complete.

1. $(\square \times 9) - 4 = 50$
2. $\square \times (9 - 4) = 50$
3. $(\square + 48) \div 4 = 15$
4. $\square + (48 \div 4) = 15$
5. $(\square \div 20) - 17 = 8$
6. $\square \div (20 - 17) = 8$
7. $(\square \times 8) + 40 = 240$
8. $\square \times (8 + 40) = 240$
9. $(\square \div 6) \times 3 = 1 \cdot 5$
10. $\square \div (6 \times 3) = 1 \cdot 5$

Place two pairs of brackets to make each calculation complete.

11. $19 \times 5 - 2 = 3 \times 14 + 17$
12. $8 + 9 \times 2 = 144 \div 6 + 2$
13. $45 + 81 \div 9 = 6 + 16 \times 3$
14. $165 - 27 \div 3 = 2 \cdot 5 \times 20 - 4$
15. $3 \times 44 - 12 = 960 \div 16 \div 2$
16. $12 + 60 \div 8 = 0 \cdot 75 + 1 \cdot 25 \times 15$
17. $6 \times 50 - 15 = 60 + 600 \div 4$
18. $90 \div 6 - 3 = 4 \cdot 5 + 2 \cdot 5 \times 3$
19. $3 - 1 \cdot 2 \times 5 = 0 \cdot 5 \times 12 - 9$
20. $12 + 75 \div 3 = 3 \times 13 - 2$

I can solve number problems using a calculator if needed.

A

Find a pair of numbers with:

1. a sum of 14 and a product of 48.

2. a sum of 13 and a product of 22.

3. a sum of 17 and a product of 70.

4. a sum of 16 and a product of 48.

5. a sum of 16 and a product of 63.

6. a sum of 30 and a product of 125.

Which number when multiplied by itself gives:

7. 64

8. 121

9. 361

10. 196

11. 400

12. 256?

Find two consecutive numbers with a product of:

13. 42

14. 110

15. 210

16. 380

17. 306

18. 600.

B

Find the number.

1. a 2-digit number a prime number the sum of its digits is 13

2. a 2-digit number a multiple of both 3 and 4 the sum of its digits is 15

3. a prime number a factor of 78 a 2-digit number

4. a 3-digit number a square number the product of its digits is 2

Which number when multiplied by itself gives:

5. 1156
8. 841

6. 4489
9. 5184

7. 2025
10. 9604?

Find two consecutive numbers with a product of:

11. 552
14. 1406

12. 702
15. 1722

13. 812
16. 4160.

17. What is the largest 2-digit number that can be multiplied by itself to give a 3-digit number?

18. Find two numbers between 30 and 40 with a product of:

a) 1254

b) 1224.

C

Find the number.

1. a square number a 3-digit number the product of its digits is 20

2. a 2-digit number a factor of 184 a prime number

3. a multiple of 11 a multiple of 7 the product of its digits is 6

4. a 3-digit number the sum of its digits is 9 a multiple of 37

Find two consecutive numbers with a product of:

5. 992

6. 1122

7. 1892

8. 2256

9. 2756

10. 8010

Find a pair of any numbers greater than 1 with a product of:

11. 115
17. 671

12. 111
18. 623

13. 287
19. 493

14. 143
20. 949

15. 395
21. 851

16. 201
22. 1007

I can use my knowledge of multiplication facts to quickly work out calculations involving decimals.

A
What is
1. 5×6
2. 3×7
3. 6×9
4. 9×5

5. 4×80
6. 7×60
7. 6×70
8. 8×40

9. 20×9
10. 50×3
11. 90×7
12. 70×8

13. $48 \div 6$
14. $48 \div 8$
15. $18 \div 2$
16. $45 \div 9$

17. $490 \div 7$
18. $240 \div 8$
19. $240 \div 4$
20. $180 \div 6$

21. $720 \div 90$
22. $210 \div 30$
23. $280 \div 70$
24. $540 \div 60$

B
Write the answer only.
1. 9×0.6
2. 4×0.9
3. 7×0.2
4. 4×0.7

5. 6×0.4
6. 8×0.8
7. 0.5×9
8. 0.8×3

9. 0.7×7
10. 0.6×5
11. 0.8×6
12. 0.3×8

13. $2.7 \div 9$
14. $1.4 \div 7$
15. $3.6 \div 4$
16. $5.6 \div 8$

17. $1.6 \div 2$
18. $1.8 \div 6$
19. $3.5 \div 5$
20. $4 \div 8$

21. $3.2 \div 4$
22. $1.5 \div 3$
23. $5.4 \div 9$
24. $3 \div 6$

Copy and complete.
25. $\square \times 6 = 5.4$
26. $\square \times 9 = 3.6$
27. $\square \times 2 = 1.4$
28. $\square \times 0.7 = 2.8$
29. $\square \times 0.4 = 2.4$
30. $\square \times 0.8 = 6.4$
31. $\square \div 9 = 0.5$
32. $\square \div 3 = 0.8$
33. $\square \div 7 = 0.7$
34. $\square \div 5 = 0.6$
35. $\square \div 6 = 0.8$
36. $\square \div 8 = 0.3$

C
Write the answer only.
1. 0.08×4
2. 0.7×6
3. 0.005×9
4. 0.06×8

5. 0.6×6
6. 0.06×9
7. 3×0.8
8. 8×0.09

9. 7×0.07
10. 8×0.5
11. 6×0.09
12. 9×0.9

13. $0.21 \div 3$
14. $0.56 \div 7$
15. $3.2 \div 8$
16. $0.64 \div 8$

17. $3.6 \div 9$
18. $0.63 \div 7$
19. $0.42 \div 6$
20. $0.81 \div 9$

21. $6.3 \div 9$
22. $0.18 \div 3$
23. $2 \div 5$
24. $5.6 \div 8$

Copy and complete.
25. $\square \times 8 = 0.48$
26. $\square \times 7 = 5.6$
27. $\square \times 5 = 0.45$
28. $\square \times 7 = 0.63$
29. $\square \times 4 = 0.28$
30. $\square \times 6 = 3.6$
31. $\square \div 8 = 0.08$
32. $\square \div 7 = 0.4$
33. $\square \div 9 = 0.09$
34. $\square \div 7 = 0.6$
35. $\square \div 6 = 0.09$
36. $\square \div 8 = 0.05$

I can work out the squares of multiples of 10.

When a number is multiplied by itself you get a square number.
They are called square numbers because they make square patterns.

$1^2 = 1 \times 1 = 1$

$2^2 = 2 \times 2 = 4$

$3^2 = 3 \times 3 = 9$

$4^2 = 4 \times 4 = 16$

A

1. Complete this table up to 12^2.
   $1^2 = 1 \times 1 = 1$
   $2^2 = 2 \times 2 = 4$
   $3^2 = 3 \times 3 = 9$

Work out

2. $4^2 + 2^2$

3. $5^2 + 3^2$

4. $6^2 + 1^2$

5. $5^2 - 3^2$

6. $8^2 - 6^2$

7. $6^2 - 3^2$

8. $10^2 + 7^2$

9. $9^2 + 1^2$

10. $8^2 + 5^2$

11. $9^2 - 4^2$

12. $10^2 - 6^2$

13. $8^2 - 7^2$

14. The factors of 4 are 1, 2 and 4.
    The factors of 9 are 1, 3 and 9.
    Find all the factors of the square numbers below 100.

B

Work out

1. 40^2
2. 70^2
3. 20^2
4. 90^2
5. 50^2
6. 80^2
7. 30^2
8. 60^2
9. 100^2
10. 120^2

Which number when multiplied by itself gives a product of:

11. 900
12. 3600
13. 100
14. 1600
15. 8100
16. 400
17. 4900
18. 2500
19. 6400
20. 10 000?

Find all the factors of these numbers.

21. 30
22. 76
23. 121
24. 58
25. 67
26. 100
27. 92
28. 144

29. What do you notice about the numbers which have an odd number of factors?

C

Find a pair of square numbers which give a total of:

1. 13
2. 125
3. 74
4. 97
5. 113
6. 4000
7. 7300
8. 18 100
9. 4100
10. 11 700.

Find a pair of square numbers which give a difference of:

11. 5
12. 19
13. 28
14. 8
15. 21
16. 5100
17. 1100
18. 1500
19. 2000
20. 5600.

21. Explain why all square numbers have an odd number of factors.

22. Explain why all numbers, other than square numbers, have an even number of factors.

I can identify the prime numbers less than 100.

A prime number is a number which is divisible by only two different numbers: by itself and by one.

The first four prime numbers are 2, 3, 5 and 7. Notice that 1 is *not* a prime number.
4, 6, 8, 9 and 10 are not prime numbers because they are divisible by at least one of the first four prime numbers.

To find out if a two-digit number is a prime number you need to work out if it is divisible by one of the first four prime numbers, 2, 3, 5 and 7.

Examples

28 is divisible by 7.   28 is not a prime number.
29 is not divisible by 2, 3, 5 or 7.   29 is a prime number.
30 is divisible by 2, 3 and 5.   30 is not a prime number.
31 is not divisible by 2, 3, 5 or 7.   31 is a prime number.

A

Write down the prime number in each group.

1. 7, 8, 9

2. 16, 17, 18

3. 21, 22, 23

4. 30, 31, 32

5. 47, 48, 49

6. 57, 58, 59

7. 66, 67, 68

8. 73, 74, 75

9. Find the next prime number:
   a) after 24
   b) after 37.

10. Find all the prime numbers below 50. There are 15. (Remember, 1 is not a prime number.)

B

Write down the two numbers in each group which are *not* prime numbers.

1. 1   11   21   31

2. 40   41   42   43

3. 33   43   53   63

4. 47   57   67   77

5. 51   61   71   81

6. 67   77   87   97

Write down the next prime number after:

7. 30

8. 45

9. 50

10. 75

11. 83

12. 93.

13. Find all the prime numbers below 100. There are 25.

14. Explain why 1038 is not a prime number.

C

In the questions in this section you may need to work out if a number is divisible by prime numbers other than 2, 3, 5 and 7.

Example

121 is not a prime number because it is divisible by 11.

Which of these are prime numbers?

1. 103

2. 111

3. 116

4. 127

5. 133

6. 139

7. 153

8. 181

9. 197

10. 182

Explain why the following are not prime numbers.

11. 74

12. 87

13. 91

14. 115

15. 143

16. 169

17. 187

18. 289

19. 247

20. 667

I can recognise and use sequences, patterns and relationships.

A

Break the second number down into factors to work out:

1. 9 × 12
2. 7 × 15
3. 17 × 9
4. 120 ÷ 8
5. 350 ÷ 14
6. 168 ÷ 12.

7. Investigate the multiples of 50. What do you notice about the last two digits?

8. Halve and halve again to test whether these numbers are divisible by 4.
   - a) 126
   - b) 148
   - c) 136
   - d) 118

Copy each sequence. Write the next 5 terms.

9. 65 69 73 77
10. 21 26 31 36
11. 86 77 68 59
12. 1 2 4 8

13. Investigate this statement.

   The difference between two successive square numbers increases by two every time.

B

Use factors to work out:

1. 24 × 15
2. 21 × 16
3. 35 × 24
4. 198 ÷ 22
5. 324 ÷ 18
6. 224 ÷ 28

7. Investigate the multiples of 25. What do you notice about the last two digits?

8. Use halving to test whether these numbers are divisible by 8.
   - a) 152
   - b) 184
   - c) 220
   - d) 312

Copy each sequence. Write the next 5 terms.

9. 18 39 60 81
10. 1 4 9 16
11. 5 30 55 80
12. 1 3 6 10

13. Investigate this statement.

   The difference between successive triangular numbers increases by one each time.

C

Use factors to work out:

1. 1·3 × 56
2. 32 × 1·5
3. 18 × 5·5
4. 40·8 ÷ 24
5. 33 ÷ 15
6. 5·85 ÷ 45

7. Investigate the multiples of 75. What do you notice about the last two digits?

8. Use halving to test whether these numbers are divisible by 16.
   - a) 400
   - b) 202
   - c) 1000
   - d) 112

Copy each sequence. Write the next 5 terms.

9. 1 50 99 148
10. 2 5 10 17
11. 100 99 97 94
12. 1 3 9 27

13. Investigate this statement.

   Any square number is the sum of two consecutive triangular numbers.

I can use my knowledge of multiples to solve problems.

Example

There are less than 40 chocolates in a box. The number of chocolates is a multiple of 4. One chocolate is eaten. The number of chocolates is now a multiple of 5. How many chocolates might there be in the box?

Method   Write out the multiples of 4 and the multiples of 5 below 40.
Look for multiples of 5 which are one less than a multiple of 4.
Multiples of 4   4   8   12   16   20   24   28   32   36
Multiples of 5   5   10   15   20   25   30   35
Possible combinations are 16, 15 and 36, 35

Answer   *There are either 16 or 36 chocolates in the box.*

A

Write the first six multiples of each of these numbers.

1. 3   4. 25
2. 7   5. 12
3. 9   6. 20

Write Yes or No.

7. Is 48 a multiple of 6?
8. Is 54 a multiple of 7?
9. Is 120 a multiple of 8?
10. Is 74 a multiple of 9?
11. Is 77 a multiple of 11?
12. Is 180 a multiple of 18?
13. Write the first ten multiples of:
    a) 3   b) 6.
14. Which numbers appear in both lists?
15. Write out all the multiples below 100 of:
    a) 10   b) 15.
16. Which numbers appear in both lists?

B

1. Chester's age is a multiple of 9. Next year it will be a multiple of 8. How old is Chester?

2. Vera has 100 books. She notices that the number of her fiction books is a multiple of 4 and of her non-fiction books is a multiple of 7. How many fiction books does Vera have and how many non-fiction books? Find all the possible solutions.

3. There are between 40 and 100 sweets in a packet. The number of sweets is a multiple of 3. If one is eaten it is a multiple of 5. How many sweets are there in the packet? Find all the possible solutions.

C

1. Ewen notices that his age, his mother's age and his grandmother's age are all multiples of 7. He also notices that in one year's time they will all be multiples of 5. How old are Ewen, his mother and his grandmother?

2. There are 60 people on a coach trip. The number of boys is a multiple of 5. The number of adults is a multiple of 4 and the number of girls is a multiple of 9. There are seven possible combinations of boys, girls and adults. Can you find them all?

3. Mr Godfrey notices that the numbers of boys, girls and adults on the coach are all multiples of 6. How many boys are on the coach?

I can identify pairs of parallel and perpendicular sides in 2-D shapes.

Example

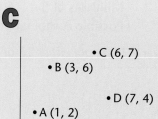

1 pair of parallel sides (shown with arrows)
2 pairs of perpendicular sides (90° angles marked)

A

Copy the following shapes. Show pairs of parallel and perpendicular sides as in the example above.

1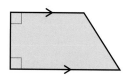

2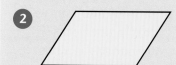

3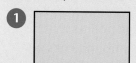

4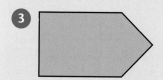

5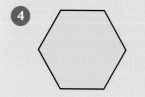

6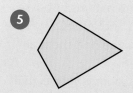

B

How many pairs of parallel sides are there in:

1 an equilateral triangle

2 a square

3 a regular pentagon

4 a regular hexagon

5 a regular heptagon

6 a regular octagon?

Predict the number of pairs of parallel sides in a regular polygon with:

7 11 sides

9 25 sides

8 10 sides

10 100 sides.

11 This pentagon has been drawn in a 3 × 3 grid.

Use 3 × 3 grids on squared or dotty paper. Make as many different polygons with more than three sides as you can. Show pairs of parallel and perpendicular lines as in the example.

C

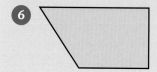

• C (6, 7)
• B (3, 6)
• D (7, 4)
• A (1, 2)

1 Draw the quadrilateral ABCD on a grid. Show any perpendicular sides.

2 Give the co-ordinates of the position to which you would move:

a) A to make a square

b) B to make a rectangle.

3 Look at the different quadrilaterals shown on page 64. What type of quadrilateral do you make if you move:

a) D to (5, 4)

b) C to (9, 8)

c) D to (10, 5)

d) A to (2, 9)?

4 On each of the six quadrilaterals in questions **2** and **3** show any parallel or perpendicular lines.

I can classify 2-D shapes using different criteria.

TRIANGLES	QUADRILATERALS		OTHER POLYGONS	
equilateral	square	parallelogram	5 sides – pentagon	CONVEX – all angles < 180°
isosceles	rectangle	kite	6 sides – hexagon	CONCAVE – 1 angle > 180°
right-angled	rhombus	trapezium	7 sides – heptagon	
scalene			8 sides – octagon	

A

1 Write the name of each shape.

A 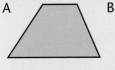   B 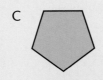   C    D   E 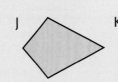   F

G 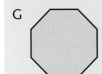   H   I   J   K 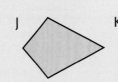   L

B

Which of the above shapes A to L are:

1 regular

2 concave

3 have more than 2 lines of symmetry

4 have one line of symmetry only?

Write down the names of two quadrilaterals with:

5 four equal sides

6 opposite sides equal and parallel

7 no right angle and opposite angles equal

8 four right angles.

Write down the name of one quadrilateral with:

9 one pair of parallel sides

10 one pair of equal opposite angles

11 equal adjacent sides.

C

Give the sum of the angles of:

1 an equilateral triangle

2 a square

3 a regular pentagon

4 a regular hexagon.

5 Write a formula for the largest number of parallel lines (p) possible in a regular shape with s sides if s is:

   a) even   **b)** odd.

6 Write a formula for the largest number of perpendicular sides (p) possible in a polygon with s sides where s is greater than 3 and:

   a) even   **b)** odd.

7 Which quadrilaterals have diagonals which:

   a) bisect   **b)** are perpendicular?

I can make and accurately draw 2-D shapes and make 3-D shapes by constructing nets or using straws.

A

1 Investigate making 2-D shapes on a 3 × 3 grid on squared or dotty paper.

Examples

How many different ways can you make an isosceles triangle, a square, a parallelogram, etc? Can you make symmetrical polygons? What is the largest number of sides a shape can have?

2 What different shapes can you make placing:

a) 3 squares side by side

b) 4 squares side by side?

3 Make a skeleton cube using art straws.

4 Make a net of a cube.

5 Use a set square and a ruler only.

a) Draw a rectangle with sides of 5 cm and 3·5 cm.

b) Draw a square with sides of 4·5 cm.

B

1 Use a large square piece of card.

a) Mark the middle points of 3 sides.

b) Draw these lines and cut out the shapes.

Investigate the 2-D shapes you can make using different combinations of the card shapes.

2 How many different shapes can you make by placing 2 equilateral triangles side by side? Investigate using 3, 4 or 5 equilateral triangles.

3 Make a skeleton tetrahedron using art straws.

4 Make a net for a tetrahedron.

5 Use a ruler and a protractor only.

a) Draw an equilateral triangle with 5·5 cm sides.

b) Draw a right-angled triangle with shorter sides of 4·2 cm and 5·6 cm. Measure the longest side.

C

1 Use a square piece of card.

a) Mark the mid points of each side.

b) Draw these lines. (The dotted lines are guide lines only.) Cut out the shapes.

Investigate the 2-D shapes you can make using different combinations of the shapes.

2 Make a skeleton octahedron using art straws.

3 Make a net for:

a) an octahedron

b) a triangular prism

c) a square based pyramid.

4 Use a ruler and a protractor only. Draw:

a) an isosceles triangle with a shortest side of 5·8 cm and two angles of 55°

b) a parallelogram with sides of 4·3 cm and 2·9 cm and angles of 73° and 107°

c) a rhombus with sides of 3·7 cm and angles of 68° and 112°.

I can read a scale accurately and convert between metric units.

A

Estimate the measurement indicated by each arrow.

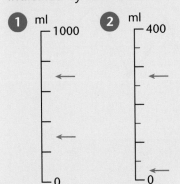

Read the measurement shown by each arrow.

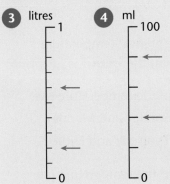

Copy and complete.

5 0·6 litres = ☐ ml

6 3·5 litres = ☐ ml

7 1200 ml = ☐ litres

8 4700 ml = ☐ litres

9 5·8 cm = ☐ mm

10 1·1 cm = ☐ mm

11 4 mm = ☐ cm

12 26 mm = ☐ cm

B

Estimate the measurement indicated by each arrow.

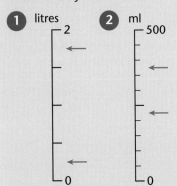

3 Match X, Y and Z to the letters on the second scale showing the equivalent measurements.

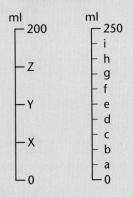

Copy and complete.

4 5·74 litres = ☐ ml

5 1·31 litres = ☐ ml

6 2030 ml = ☐ litres

7 3290 ml = ☐ litres

8 0·87 m = ☐ cm

9 4·18 m = ☐ cm

10 162 cm = ☐ m

11 645 cm = ☐ m

C

Estimate the measurement indicated by each arrow.

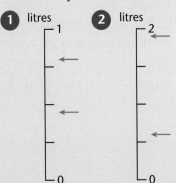

3 Match X, Y and Z to the letters on the second scale showing the equivalent measurements.

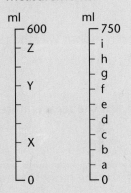

Copy and complete.

4 2·417 litres = ☐ ml

5 0·293 litres = ☐ ml

6 1965 ml = ☐ litres

7 5321 ml = ☐ litres

8 4·734 km = ☐ m

9 0·858 km = ☐ m

10 1589 g = ☐ kg

11 3145 g = ☐ kg

I can construct and interpret line graphs.

Line graphs are graphs in which a set of data is plotted and the points are joined up with a line. Line graphs often show a trend.

Example
This line graph shows the average daily maximum temperature in Sweden.

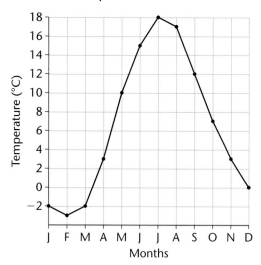

In which month was the temperature 3°C?
April

What was the temperature in October?
7°C

What was the highest temperature?
18°C

What was the lowest temperature?
−3°C

What was the range in temperature?
21°C (from 18°C to −3°C)

A

This line graph shows the highest temperature recorded each day in one week in November.

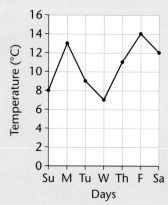

1 On which day was the temperature 11°C?

2 What was the highest temperature on Saturday?

3 What was the highest temperature recorded during the week?

4 How much did the temperature rise:
   a) between Sunday and Monday
   b) between Thursday and Friday?

5 How much did the temperature fall:
   a) between Monday and Tuesday
   b) between Tuesday and Wednesday?

6 Use this table to draw a line graph showing the lowest temperatures recorded daily in the same week.

Days	Lowest Temperature (°C)
Sunday	3
Monday	5
Tuesday	0
Wednesday	−2
Thursday	2
Friday	4
Saturday	7

B

This line graph shows the average daily maximum temperature in Leeds during one year.

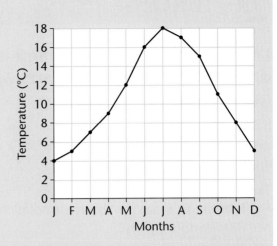

1 What was the temperature in August?

2 In which month was the temperature 9°C?

3 Between which two months was there:

    a) the largest rise in temperature

    b) the largest fall in temperature?

4 What was the range in temperature?

5 Use the table below to draw a line graph showing the temperature on one day in November.

Time	0400	0600	0800	1000	1200	1400	1600	1800	2000	2200	0000	0200	0400
Temperature (°C)	0	−2	−1	3	8	11	10	7	5	3	2	1	0

6 Use your graph to estimate the temperature at 0900.

7 Use your graph to estimate how long the temperature was below 0°C.

C

This line graph shows the depth of water in a stream.

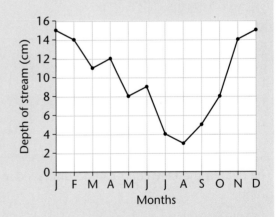

1 How deep was the stream in March?

2 In which two months was the stream 8 cm deep?

3 Which month saw the largest increase in depth? Why do you think this happened?

4 What was the range of the depths?

5 For how long was the stream below 4 cm deep?

6 Use the table to draw a line graph to show the height of a plane during a training flight.

Flight Time (minutes)	0	10	20	30	40	50	60	70	80	90	100	110	120
Height (m)	0	350	500	600	650	750	850	800	800	550	450	200	0

7 Use the graph to estimate the height of the plane 45 minutes after take off.

8 Use the graph to estimate the length of time the plane was above 500 m.

I can use frequency tables and draw and interpret bar charts with grouped data.

If the spread of a set of data is too large it is usually necessary to group the data before displaying it in the form of a graph.

Example

The ages of Mrs Evans' family on the occasion of her 100th birthday party.

78	18	1	35	26	9
54	32	45	15	11	59
39	42	0	33	21	74
6	28	48	7	24	12
100	57	37	3	81	60

A tally chart showing the grouped ages.

Age	Tally	Frequency
0–19	⳾⳾⳾⳾ ⳾⳾⳾⳾	10
20–39	⳾⳾⳾⳾ ⳾⳾⳾⳾	9
40–59	⳾⳾⳾⳾ ⳾	6
69–79	⳾⳾⳾	3
80–99	⳾	1
100+	⳾	1
Total		30

The data in the tally chart can be displayed in a graph.

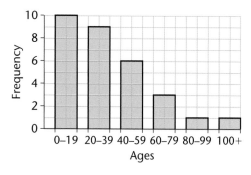

1 This bar chart shows the ages of children in a skate boarding competition.

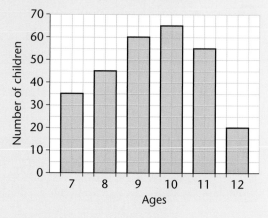

a) How many children were 9?

b) How many children were 11?

c) What was the age of the oldest child?

d) How many children were younger than 9?

e) How many children were older than 9?

f) How many children were there at the skate boarding competition?

2 The marks achieved by Class 6 in their weekly spelling test are below.

8	9	10	9	7	8	9	10
9	6	8	10	9	10	7	9
10	9	7	8	10	1	9	8
9	10	8	6	9	10	8	9

Make a frequency table and then display the data in a bar chart or a bar line chart.

B

1 This bar chart shows the percentage marks achieved by a class in a test.

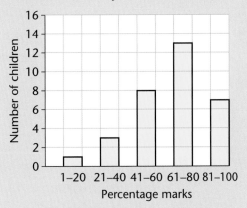

a) How many children scored below 61%?

b) How many children scored more than 40%?

c) How many children took the test?

d) What proportion of the children scored less than 41%?

e) What proportion of the children scored more than 40% and less than 61%?

2 Draw a graph to show how you think the marks would have been distributed if the same children had taken the test:

a) one term earlier

b) one term later.

3 The number of books borrowed from the School Library by the children in Year 6 in one term.

21 29 19 14 25 10 23 18 16 12
24 18 5 22 14 16 28 19 15 23
11 21 17 20 24 15 20 8 18 25
20 14 23 17 26 19 22 16 13 17

Group the data in sets of 5.
(1–5, 6–10, etc.).

Make a tally chart and then display the data in a bar chart.

C

1 This bar chart shows the distance children in one school have to travel each morning coming to school.

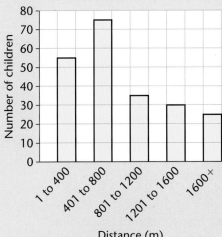

a) How many children live nearer to School than 401 m?

b) How many children live further from the School than 800 m?

c) How many children are there in the School?

d) Anjalia says

One quarter of the children in the School live more than 1200 m from the School.

Is she right? Explain your answer.

e) What proportion of the children travel more than 400 m and less than 1201 m each morning?

2 The children in Year 7 took the following numbers of minutes to travel to their new school.

43 29 6 32 12 35 53 25 47 19
17 37 15 23 52 48 20 38 4 27
26 58 44 11 22 9 31 45 36 13
56 39 25 8 48 40 51 19 30 31
24 14 50 37 55 26 18 35 7 33

Group the data.

Make a tally chart and then display the data in a bar chart.

I can interpret pie charts.

Examples

a) The favourite colours of 80 children.

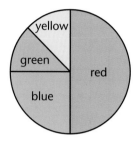

How many children chose red?
40 (80 ÷ 2)

How many children chose blue?
20 (80 ÷ 4)

Estimate the proportion of children who chose yellow.
one eighth

b) The 300 members of the audience at a film performance.

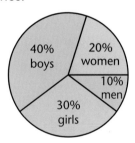

How many men were in the audience?
30 (10% of 300)

How many girls were in the audience?
90 (30% of 300)

A

1 The pie chart shows the results of the 20 games played by the school football team.

How many games were

a) won   **b)** lost   **c)** drawn?

2 The pie chart shows the 50 passengers travelling on a bus.

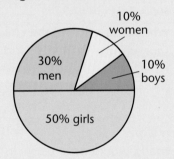

How many of the passengers were:

a) women   **b)** men   **c)** children?

3 The pie chart shows the 60 competitors at an Athletics Meeting.

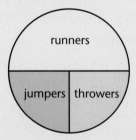

How many of the competitors were:

a) runners   **b)** jumpers   **c)** throwers?

B

1 The pie chart shows the 48 votes for the Year 6 School Council candidates.

How many votes did each candidate receive?

2 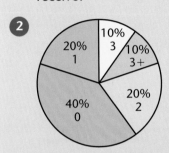 The pie chart shows the numbers of passengers in 200 cars.

Copy and complete the table.

Passengers	Cars
0	
1	
2	
3	
3+	

3 The pie chart shows the holiday destinations of 400 tourists.

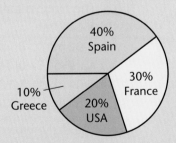

How many tourists were travelling to each country?

C

1 The pie chart below shows how the children at one school travel to school each day.

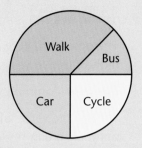

70 children cycle. Estimate:

a) how many children travel by bus

b) how many children travel by car

c) how many children walk

d) how many children there are in the school.

2 In a survey 60 adults and 80 children were asked to choose their favourite shop in a new shopping mall.
The results are shown in the pie charts.

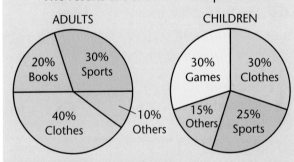

a) How many children chose games shops?

b) How many adults chose book shops?

c) Did more adults or children choose clothes shops?
Explain your answer.

d) Did more adults or children choose sports shops?
Explain your answer.

I can find the range, mode, median and mean of a set of numbers.

Example

The marks of 9 children in a test are as follows: 8 4 7 1 8 9 3 8 6

THE RANGE	The difference between the highest and lowest values.	Highest − Lowest = 9 − 1 The range is 8 marks.
THE MODE	The most common value.	mode = 8 (three times)
THE MEDIAN	The middle value when the numbers are in size order.	1 3 4 6 (7) 8 8 8 9 The median is 7.
THE MEAN	The total divided by the number of items in the set.	Total marks ÷ number of children The mean is 6. (54 ÷ 9)

A

For each of the following sets of data find:

a) the range

b) the mode

c) the median.

1 The ages of five friends.

11 9 7 11 10

2 The goals scored by 11 footballers in one season.

0   2   1   0   1   7
3   12   4   1   2

3 The daily maximum temperatures recorded in one week in March.

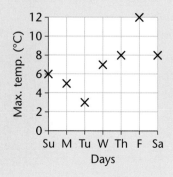

B

For each of the following sets of data find:

a) the range

b) the mode

c) the median

d) the mean.

1 The ages of 15 children at a birthday party.

2 5 7 3 4 3 6 3
2 3 5 6 4 5 2

2 The lengths in minutes of phone calls made by a bank manager.

3 2 8 4 3 12 5
7 15 3 10 2 4

3 The daily maximum temperatures recorded in one week in May.

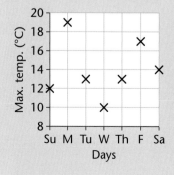

C

For each of the following sets of data find:

a) the range

b) the mode

c) the median

d) the mean.

1 The times in a 100 m sprint in seconds.

10·03   10·01   9·89
10·04   9·97   10·06
10·02   9·94   10·04

2 The heights jumped by 8 children.

1·00 m   0·96 m
1·05 m   0·74 m
1·04 m   1·12 m
0·89 m   0·96 m

3 The daily maximum temperatures recorded in one week in January.

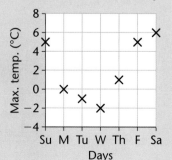

I can use a benchmark to help estimate lengths.

A

Hayley knows the door is about 2 metres tall. She estimates some distances in door lengths.

1. Write down the missing estimates, a, b and c.

2. Write down the missing door lengths, d, e and f.

3. Use this method to estimate some distances in your school. Measure the distances to check the accuracy of your results.

DISTANCE ESTIMATED	DOOR LENGTHS	ESTIMATED DISTANCE
length of Classroom	6	a
width of Classroom	4	b
length of Hall	12	c
width of Hall	d	16 m
length of Library	e	6 m
length of Corridor	f	30 m

B

Laith knows his pencil is about 20 cm long. He estimates some measurements in pencil lengths.

LENGTHS ESTIMATED	PENCIL LENGTHS	ESTIMATED LENGTH
table (length)	7	a
tray unit (length)	3	b
display board (width)	11	c
window (height)	d	2·4 m
radiator (length)	e	1·8 m
mat (length)	f	80 cm

1. Write down the missing estimates, a, b and c.

2. Write down the missing pencil lengths, d, e and f.

3. Use this method to estimate the lengths of some objects in your classroom. Measure the lengths to check the accuracy of your results.

C

Anhar knows the length of his stride is about 60 cm. He estimates some distances by counting his paces.

1. Write down the missing estimates.

2. Write down the missing number of paces.

3. Use this method to estimate some distances in your school. Measure the distances to check the accuracy of your results.

DISTANCE	PACES	ESTIMATED DISTANCE
Playground (length)	80	a
Playground (width)	48	b
Pond (perimeter)	39	c
Classroom to Hall	d	27·6 m
Classroom to Toilet	e	15 m
Classroom to Office	f	40·2 m

I can read scales accurately and compare readings from different scales.

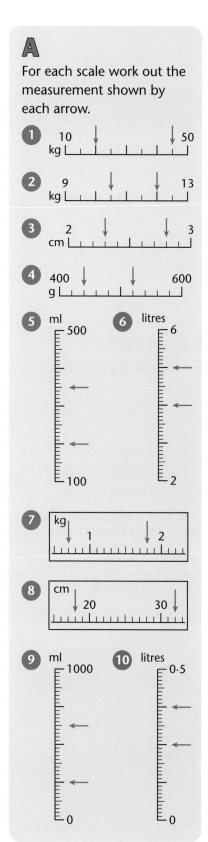

A

For each scale work out the measurement shown by each arrow.

1   10 ↓   ↓50
    kg

2   9   ↓   ↓   13
    kg

3   2   ↓   ↓   3
    cm

4 400 ↓   ↓   600
   g

5 ml
6 litres

7 kg

8 cm

9 ml
10 litres

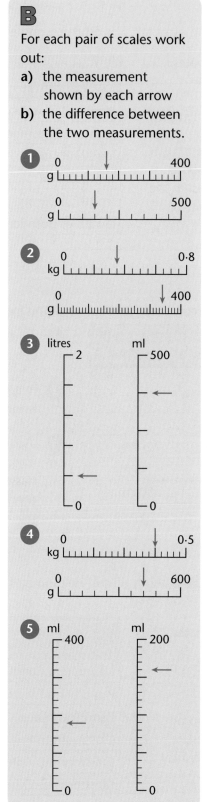

B

For each pair of scales work out:
a) the measurement shown by each arrow
b) the difference between the two measurements.

1   0   ↓   400
    g

     0   ↓   500
    g

2   0   ↓   0.8
    kg

     0   ↓ 400
    g

3 litres   ml

4   0   ↓   0.5
    kg

     0   ↓   600
    g

5 ml   ml

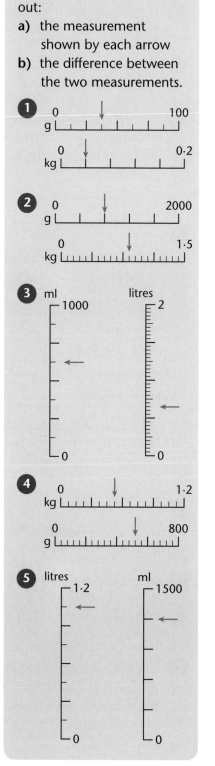

C

For each pair of scales work out:
a) the measurement shown by each arrow
b) the difference between the two measurements.

1   0   ↓   100
    g

     0 ↓   0.2
    kg

2   0   ↓   2000
    g

     0   ↓   1.5
    kg

3 ml   litres

4   0   ↓   1.2
    kg

     0   ↓   800
    g

5 litres   ml

I can convert between units of measurement.

UNITS OF LENGTH

×1000 → ×100 → ×10 →
km   m   cm   mm
← ÷1000   ÷100   ÷10

UNITS OF MASS

×1000 →
kg   g
← ÷1000

UNITS OF CAPACITY

×1000 →
litres   ml
← ÷1000

A

Copy and complete.

1. 2000 m = ☐ km
2. 3500 m = ☐ km
3. 2·5 km = ☐ m
4. 7·400 km = ☐ m
5. 290 cm = ☐ m
6. 147 cm = ☐ m
7. 3·61 m = ☐ cm
8. 0·87 m = ☐ cm
9. 37 mm = ☐ cm
10. 16 mm = ☐ cm
11. 9 cm = ☐ mm
12. 0·4 cm = ☐ mm

13. 3·4 kg = ☐ g
14. 0·17 kg = ☐ g
15. 3100 g = ☐ kg
16. 2250 g = ☐ kg

17. 0·5 litres = ☐ ml
18. 2·9 litres = ☐ ml
19. 1800 ml = ☐ litres
20. 600 ml = ☐ litres

Write in hours and minutes.

21. 4·25 hours
22. 2·5 hours
23. 1·75 hours
24. 3·5 hours

B

Copy and complete.

1. 392 m = ☐ km
2. 2756 m = ☐ km
3. 1·437 km = ☐ m
4. 0·026 km = ☐ m
5. 240 cm = ☐ m
6. 6 cm = ☐ m
7. 0·48 m = ☐ cm
8. 13·96 m = ☐ cm
9. 21 mm = ☐ m
10. 685 mm = ☐ m
11. 0·007 m = ☐ mm
12. 6·937 m = ☐ mm

13. 6·149 kg = ☐ g
14. 4·25 kg = ☐ g
15. 1593 g = ☐ kg
16. 800 g = ☐ kg

17. 1·25 litres = ☐ ml
18. 4·6 litres = ☐ ml
19. 2470 ml = ☐ litres
20. 680 ml = ☐ litres

Write in hours and minutes.

21. 1·2 hours
22. 3·7 hours
23. 8·1 hours
24. 5·9 hours

C

Copy and complete by putting >, < or = in the box.

1. 8417 mm ☐ 84·17 m
2. 23·1 cm ☐ 0·231 m
3. 7 ml ☐ 0·007 litres
4. 2460 cm ☐ 0·024 km
5. 5000 mm ☐ 0·05 km
6. 200 g ☐ 0·02 kg

7. A slug slides 125 cm every hour. How long would it take the slug to slide 0·1 km?

8. A tube of toothpaste holds 75 ml. How many tubes can be filled from 3 litres?

9. A bar of soap weighs 200 g. What is the weight of 48 bars in kilograms?

10. Trees are planted every 8 metres along the bank of a canal. There are 196 trees. How long is the canal?

I can convert imperial units to their approximate metric equivalents and vice versa.

These are the most commonly used imperial units and their metric equivalents.
(The sign ≈ means *is approximately equal to*.)

LENGTH
1 inch ≈ 2·5 cm
1 foot ≈ 30 cm
1 yard ≈ 90 cm
1 mile ≈ 1·6 km
8 km ≈ 5 miles

MASS
1 ounce ≈ 30 g
1 kg ≈ 2·2 pounds
CAPACITY
1 pint ≈ 0·6 litres
1 gallon ≈ 4·5 litres

A

Which imperial unit would you use to measure:

1. an armchair's width
2. a jug's capacity
3. a football pitch's length
4. the weight of 8 apples
5. a finger's length
6. a CD's weight
7. a motorway's length
8. a bath's capacity?

Copy and complete

9. 2 inches ≈ ☐ cm
10. 3 feet ≈ ☐ cm
11. 5 ounces ≈ ☐ g
12. 10 pints ≈ ☐ litres
13. 2 gallons ≈ ☐ litres
14. 10 miles ≈ ☐ km
15. 2 yards ≈ ☐ cm
16. 6·6 pounds ≈ ☐ kg
17. 10 cm ≈ ☐ inches
18. 45 litres ≈ ☐ gallons
19. 80 km ≈ ☐ miles
20. 9 m ≈ ☐ yards

B

Choose the best estimate.

1. a tin of beans
   1, 11 or 100 ounces
2. a bed's length
   4, 6 or 8 feet
3. London to Manchester
   2, 20 or 200 miles
4. a car's petrol tank
   10, 100 or 1000 gallons

Copy and complete.

5. 6 inches ≈ ☐ cm
6. 5 feet ≈ ☐ cm
7. 100 yards ≈ ☐ m
8. 25 miles ≈ ☐ km
9. 12 ounces ≈ ☐ g
10. 11 pounds ≈ ☐ kg
11. 6 pints ≈ ☐ litres
12. 4 gallons ≈ ☐ litres
13. 30 cm ≈ ☐ inches
14. 48 km ≈ ☐ miles
15. 240 g ≈ ☐ ounces
16. 36 litres ≈ ☐ gallons

C

Copy and complete by putting > or < in the box.

1. 15 pounds ☐ 6 kg
2. 3 yards ☐ 3 m
3. 6 feet ☐ 1 m 90 cm
4. 6 miles ☐ 12 km
5. 8 ounces ☐ 225 g
6. 6 gallons ☐ 25 litres
7. 8 yards ☐ 7 m
8. 9 feet ☐ 2 m 60 cm
9. 12 pounds ☐ 5 kg
10. 9 gallons ☐ 42 litres
11. 12 ounces ☐ 370 g
12. 11 miles ☐ 20 km
13. 5 pints ☐ 2·5 litres
14. 4 inches ☐ 11 cm
15. 8 pints ☐ 4 litres
16. 100 yards ☐ 95 m
17. Rewrite Questions 1 to 4 in Section B, changing each measurement to the approximate metric equivalent.

I can solve multi-step problems involving measures.

Example

Cherries cost £3·60 for 1 kg.
What will 225 g cost?

100 g costs 36p (£3·60 ÷ 10)
200 g costs 72p (36p × 2)
25 g costs 9p (36p ÷ 4)
225 g costs 81p (72p + 9p)

A

1. The combined weight of two babies is 18 kg. Tammy weighs 0·8 kg more than Simon. How much does each baby weigh?

2. A sachet of shampoo holds 25 ml. There are 12 sachets in one box. How much shampoo is there in five boxes?

3. A rectangle has a perimeter of 20 cm. Its longest side is 6 cm. What is its area?

4. A fish bowl contains 1500 ml of water. 25 ml evaporates. 150 ml is added. How much water is in the bowl now?

5. Nuts cost 80p for 100 g. How much will 250 g cost?

B

1. How many hours and minutes will it take Davina to type 9000 words at 60 words per minute?

2. The temperature is 4·7°C. It falls 8·65°C. It rises 2·9°C. What is the new temperature?

3. David swims 800 m every day. The pool is 50 m in length. How many lengths does he swim in one week?

4. Marsha has 132 books. They are divided equally between three shelves. Each book weighs 0·2 kg. How much weight does each shelf support?

5. Ryan fills a bath with 22·6 litres of hot water and 18·7 litres of cold. He spills 2·5 litres getting in. How much water is in the bath now?

C

1. There are 60 kitchen towels in one roll. Each towel is 22·8 cm long. What is the total length of the towels in a pack of 15 rolls?

2. A horse trough holds 12·34 litres. Dobbin drinks 0·7 litres. Beauty drinks 875 ml. How much water is left?

3. A Weetabix weighs 25 g. A large box contains four packets of 18 biscuits. What do the biscuits in the box weigh?

4. The perimeter of a square playground is 120 metres. What is the area of the playground?

5. Bird seed costs £1·60 for 1 kg. What does 425 g cost?

6. Rex and Rover eat 1·25 kg of dog food between them. Rex eats 120 g more than Rover. How much does each dog eat?

I can estimate the area of irregular shapes by counting squares and I can work out the area of shapes that can be split into rectangles.

Examples

Estimate the area of an irregular shape by counting squares on a grid. Count the square if half or more of the square is within the shape.

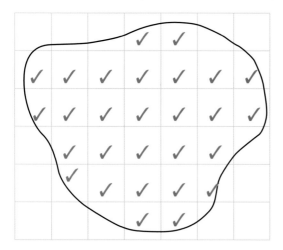

Area is about 28 cm².

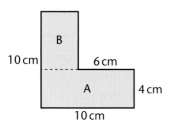

Area of A = (10 × 4) cm²
　　　　　 = 40 cm²

Area of B = (6 × 4) cm²
　　　　　 = 24 cm²

Area of L-shape = (40 + 24) cm²
　　　　　　　　 = 64 cm²

A

1 Each square on the map represents 1 square kilometre. Estimate the area of each island.

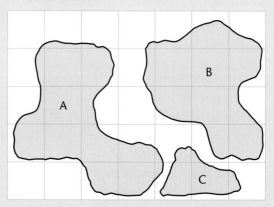

2 Copy and complete the table showing the measurements of rectangles.

Length	Width	Perimeter	Area
9 cm	7 cm		
8 cm	3 cm		
6 cm			12 cm²
12 cm			60 cm²
	6 cm	26 cm	
	8 cm	34 cm	

Use 1 cm² paper.

3 Draw three different rectangles each with an area of 36 cm².
Work out the perimeters.

4 Draw three different rectangles each with a perimeter of 36 cm.
Work out the areas.

5 Draw as many L-shapes as you can with an area of 8 cm².
Work out the perimeters.

B

1 Estimate the area of this shape.

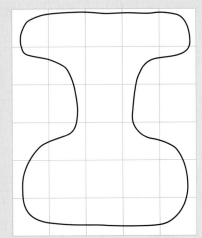

2 Use 1 cm² paper. Estimate the area of your hand.

For each of the following shapes work out:

a) the perimeter

b) the area.

All lengths are in centimetres.

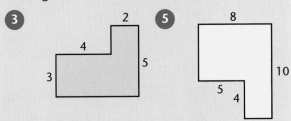

Use 1 cm² paper.

7 Draw two different L-shapes with an area of 20 cm.
Work out the perimeter of each shape.

8 Draw two different T-shapes with a perimeter of 20 cm.
Work out the area of each shape.

C

For each shape work out:

a) the perimeter

b) the area.

All lengths are in centimetres.

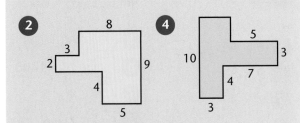

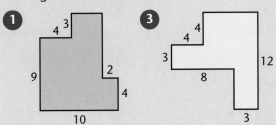

5 Use 1 cm² paper. Estimate the area of your foot.

6 How many square millimetres are there in one square centimetre?

7 How many square centimetres are there in one square metre?

8 How many square millimetres are there in one square metre?

9 A room is 5 metres long by 3 metres wide. It costs £285 to carpet the room. How much does the carpet cost per square metre?

10 Each wall tile is 20 cm by 20 cm. How many tiles are needed to cover

a) one square metre

b) the area of bathroom wall shown below?

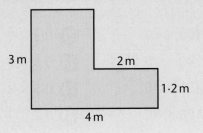

I can use multiplication facts to find related facts involving decimals.

A

What is

1. 7×2
2. 5×7
3. 8×9
4. 3×6

5. 6×50
6. 9×80
7. 7×30
8. 9×40

9. 20×8
10. 60×6
11. 40×9
12. 70×7

13. $32 \div 8$
14. $24 \div 3$
15. $81 \div 9$
16. $30 \div 6$

17. $210 \div 7$
18. $450 \div 5$
19. $240 \div 4$
20. $560 \div 8$

21. $480 \div 60$
22. $180 \div 20$
23. $420 \div 70$
24. $180 \div 90$

B

Copy and complete.

1. $\square \times 8 = 64$
2. $\square \times 9 = 54$
3. $\square \times 3 = 2700$
4. $\square \times 5 = 400$

5. $\square \times 60 = 240$
6. $\square \times 70 = 1400$
7. $\square \div 9 = 5$
8. $\square \div 2 = 6$

9. $\square \div 8 = 300$
10. $\square \div 70 = 90$
11. $\square \div 4 = 80$
12. $\square \div 600 = 7$

Write the answer only.

13. 4×0.7
14. 8×0.2
15. 2×0.6
16. 6×0.3

17. 7×0.9
18. 6×0.8
19. 0.7×5
20. 0.9×6

21. 0.3×9
22. 0.8×7
23. 0.5×8
24. 0.7×4

25. $1.5 \div 5$
26. $3.6 \div 9$
27. $1.4 \div 2$
28. $4.9 \div 7$

29. $1.6 \div 8$
30. $3 \div 6$
31. $2.4 \div 0.4$
32. $1.5 \div 0.3$

33. $2.1 \div 0.7$
34. $7.2 \div 0.9$
35. $3 \div 0.6$
36. $4 \div 0.5$

C

Copy and complete.

1. $\square \times 7 = 4.2$
2. $\square \times 5 = 0.45$
3. $\square \times 0.8 = 0.56$
4. $\square \times 0.9 = 4.5$

5. $\square \times 0.3 = 0.24$
6. $\square \times 0.6 = 1.2$
7. $\square \div 2 = 0.8$
8. $\square \div 8 = 0.3$

9. $\square \div 9 = 0.09$
10. $\square \div 0.7 = 4$
11. $\square \div 0.6 = 80$
12. $\square \div 0.4 = 0.9$

Write the answer only.

13. 7×0.9
14. 6×0.03
15. 0.4×8
16. 0.8×0.4

17. 0.9×6
18. 0.07×5
19. 5×0.7
20. 6×0.08

21. 0.4×0.9
22. 0.08×7
23. 0.9×2
24. 3×0.06

25. $0.64 \div 0.08$
26. $1.4 \div 7$
27. $30 \div 0.5$
28. $2.4 \div 0.6$

29. $5.4 \div 9$
30. $0.27 \div 3$
31. $6.3 \div 0.7$
32. $12 \div 0.2$

33. $0.42 \div 6$
34. $4 \div 8$
35. $28 \div 0.4$
36. $7.2 \div 0.9$

I can solve number problems and puzzles.

A

1 | 3 | 4 | 5 |

Use the above digits once only. Place one digit in each box so that the answer is a whole number. Find both possible solutions.

□ · □ × □

2 | 2 | 4 | 5 | 6 |

Use the above digits once only. Place one digit in each box to make:

a) the smallest possible answer

b) the largest possible answer.

□ □ □ ÷ □

Copy and complete.

3 □ + 0·25 = 7

4 □ − 3·8 = 4·5

5 1·2 × □ = 6

6 4·2 ÷ □ = 0·42

Which number multiplied by itself gives:

7 64   **9** 400

8 121   **10** 225?

Find two numbers:

11 with a sum of 37 and a difference of 3

12 with a sum of 56 and a difference of 12.

B

1 | 2 | 5 | 7 | 8 |

Use the above digits once only. Place one digit in each box so that the answer is a whole number. Find all possible solutions.

□ □ · □ × □

2 | 1 | 2 | 3 | 4 |

Use the above digits once only. Place one digit in each box to make:

a) the smallest possible product

b) the largest possible product.

□ □ × □ □

Copy and complete.

3 □ + 1·48 = 3·11

4 □ − 4·08 = 12·035

5 23·75 × □ = 109·25

6 784·3 ÷ □ = 68·2

Find two numbers between 20 and 30 with a product of:

7 675

8 667.

Find two numbers:

9 with a sum of 123 and a difference of 25

10 with a sum of 6 and a difference of 0·3.

C

Copy and complete.

1 (□ + 5·38) ÷ 4 = 3·6

2 (□ − 1·35) × 12 = 9

3 (□ ÷ 1·2) − 0·38 = 4·62

4 (□ × 7) + 0·6 = 30

Find the number that lies halfway between:

5 5·74 and 6·3

6 4·1 and 3·29.

Find two consecutive numbers with a product of:

7 306   **9** 2652

8 1260   **10** 6162.

Find three consecutive numbers with a total of:

11 81   **13** 291

12 168   **14** 552.

Copy and complete

15 □7 × 4□ = 4263

16 1748 ÷ □3 = 7□

17 The perimeter of a square is 96 cm. What is its area?

18 The area of a square is 1024 cm². What is its perimeter?

I can divide decimal numbers by one-digit whole numbers.

Examples

a) $21{\cdot}6 \div 4$

Estimate first

$4 \times 5{\cdot}0 = 20{\cdot}0$

$4 \times 6{\cdot}0 = 24{\cdot}0$

$20{\cdot}0 < 21{\cdot}6 < 24{\cdot}0$

$5{\cdot}0 <$ Answer $< 6{\cdot}0$

```
   21.6
 − 20.0   (4 × 5.0)
 ──────
    1.6
 −  1.6   (4 × 0.4)
 ──────
      0
```
Answer 5·4

b) $178 \div 5$

```
   178
 − 150   (5 × 30)
 ─────
    28
 −  25   (5 × 5)
 ─────
   3.0
   3.0   (5 × 0.6)
 ─────
     0
```
Answer 35·6

c) $17{\cdot}8 \div 5$

```
   17.8
 − 15.0   (5 × 3.0)
 ──────
    2.8
 −  2.5   (5 × 0.5)
 ──────
    0.3
 −  0.3   (5 × 0.06)
 ──────
      0
```
Answer 3·56

A

Work out

1 $19{\cdot}2 \div 3$ 9 $24{\cdot}5 \div 5$

2 $25{\cdot}6 \div 4$ 10 $49{\cdot}6 \div 8$

3 $32{\cdot}5 \div 5$ 11 $33{\cdot}6 \div 6$

4 $37{\cdot}6 \div 4$ 12 $29{\cdot}1 \div 3$

5 $46{\cdot}8 \div 6$ 13 $54{\cdot}6 \div 7$

6 $15{\cdot}8 \div 2$ 14 $38{\cdot}4 \div 8$

7 $32{\cdot}9 \div 7$ 15 $70{\cdot}2 \div 9$

8 $29{\cdot}7 \div 9$ 16 $55{\cdot}8 \div 6$

17 Liam's father weighs 75·6 kg. Liam weighs half as much. What is Liam's weight?

18 Edie cycles 20·4 km in one hour. How far does she cycle in 10 minutes?

19 A rope is 63·6 metres long. It is cut into four equal lengths. How long is each length?

B

Work out to one decimal place.

1 $53 \div 2$ 5 $254 \div 4$

2 $178 \div 4$ 6 $172 \div 8$

3 $241 \div 5$ 7 $423 \div 5$

4 $169 \div 2$ 8 $107 \div 2$

Work out to two decimal places.

9 $2{\cdot}6 \div 4$ 13 $8{\cdot}2 \div 4$

10 $5{\cdot}4 \div 5$ 14 $7{\cdot}9 \div 5$

11 $6{\cdot}8 \div 8$ 15 $3{\cdot}5 \div 2$

12 $9{\cdot}1 \div 2$ 16 $7{\cdot}6 \div 8$

17 Five bags of cement weigh 43 kg. How much does one bag weigh?

18 Spike has 10 litres of paint. He uses one eighth. How much paint is left in litres?

C

Work out to two decimal places.

1 $63 \div 4$ 5 $86 \div 8$

2 $97 \div 4$ 6 $30 \div 8$

3 $35 \div 4$ 7 $58 \div 8$

4 $19 \div 4$ 8 $102 \div 8$

Work out to three decimal places.

9 $1{\cdot}73 \div 2$ 13 $0{\cdot}45 \div 6$

10 $9{\cdot}4 \div 4$ 14 $7{\cdot}5 \div 4$

11 $0{\cdot}37 \div 5$ 15 $0{\cdot}31 \div 5$

12 $2{\cdot}68 \div 8$ 16 $2{\cdot}6 \div 8$

17 A racing car completes four laps of a circuit. The milometer records 13·3 miles. How long is one lap?

18 A cake weighs 1·2 kg. It is cut into eight equal slices. What is the weight of one slice in kilograms?

I can solve word problems using an efficient written method.

Example

Rebecca is cycling 18·6 km.
She has travelled one
quarter of the distance.
How far has she gone?

$$
\begin{array}{r}
4\,\overline{)\,18\cdot6} \\
-16\cdot0 \quad (4 \times 4\cdot0) \\
\hline
2\cdot6 \\
-\ 2\cdot4 \quad (4 \times 0\cdot6) \\
\hline
0\cdot2 \\
-\ 0\cdot2 \quad (4 \times 0\cdot05) \\
\hline
0
\end{array}
$$

Answer = 4·65
Rebecca cycled 4·65 km.

A

1. Joanne runs a bath using 36·5 litres of hot water and 24·38 litres of cold. How much water is now in the bath?

2. The total weight of six boxes is 162 kg. What is the mean weight?

3. Neil weighs 84·7 kg. June weighs 36·4 kg less. What does June weigh?

4. James' new pair of football boots normally cost £47·50 but there is 10% off in a sale. How much does James pay?

5. A bucket holds 6·3 litres of water. The water from a butt fills the bucket eight times. How much water was in the butt?

B

1. There is 13·8 kg of potatoes in a bag. One quarter is used. How much is left?

2. There is 9·58 litres of water in an aquarium. David adds 0·625 litres. How much water is now in the aquarium?

3. One gallon is 4·55 litres. A barrel holds 6 gallons. What is this in litres?

4. A fence is 16·4 m long. 30% is painted. How long is the unpainted fence?

5. A beach pony walks a 0·35 km circuit 17 times. How far does she walk altogether?

6. What is 22% of 5·8 km?

7. Alison always gives 5% of her earnings to charity. In one week she earns £678. How much does she give?

C

1. A square field has a perimeter of 1·94 km. How long is each side?

2. Three packed cases weigh 26·74 kg, 39·6 kg and 15·392 kg. What is the mean weight of the cases?

3. Eight identical glasses are filled from 1·88 litres of drink. What is the capacity of each glass?

4. A roll of cloth is 10 m long. Lengths of 2·7 m, 58 cm and 1264 mm are cut off. How much cloth is left?

5. One can weighs 0·825 kg. What do 16 cans weigh?

6. Lasith weighs 85·4 kg. He reduces his weight by 3%. What does he weigh now?

7. Lloyd saves £9·50 each week. How long will it take him to save £228?

I can work systematically to solve a problem.

A new town is planned. All the roads will run either east–west or north–south. Each road will cross at least one other road. Traffic lights will be set up at every road junction.

When 4 roads have been built either 3 or 4 sets of traffic lights are needed.

 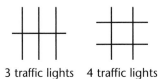

3 traffic lights   4 traffic lights

A

Look at the above information.

1. How many traffic lights might be needed for 5 roads? Find both answers.

2. How many traffic lights might be needed for 6 roads? Find 3 possible answers.

3. Debra has 2ps and 5ps only. She has 26p altogether. How many 2ps does she have and how many 5ps? Find both possible answers.

4. Keith also has 2ps and 5ps only. He has 39p. How many 2ps does he have and how many 5ps? There are four possible answers.

B

Look at the above information.
Find the minimum and the maximum number of traffic lights needed for:

1. 7 roads
2. 8 roads
3. 9 roads
4. 10 roads.

5. Martian creatures are either tripods or octopods. Tripods have three legs. Octopods have eight legs. The Martians, on an exploratory visit to Earth, have 60 legs between them. How many are tripods and how many are octopods? Find both possible solutions.

C

Look at the above information.
Find the minimum and the maximum number of traffic lights needed for:

1. 20 roads
2. 100 roads.

Write a formula for:

3. the maximum number of traffic lights needed (T) for n roads

4. the minimum number of traffic lights needed (t) for n roads.

5. How many traffic lights might be needed for 12 roads. Find all the possible solutions.

6. An orange drink costs 60p. A cola costs 70p. Some children buy orange and cola drinks for exactly £10. How many orange drinks are bought and how many colas? Find both possible solutions.

I can write a quotient as a fraction and a larger whole number as a fraction of a smaller one.

Examples

$24 \div 7 = 3\frac{3}{7}$

How many times larger is 7 than 3?

⬤⬤⬤ ⬤⬤⬤ ⬤
⬤⬤⬤

7 is $2\frac{1}{3}$ times larger than 3.

How many times larger is £60 than £8?

$60 \div 8 = 7\frac{4}{8} = 7\frac{1}{2}$

£60 is $7\frac{1}{2}$ times larger than £8.

Simplify fractions

$26 \div 8 = 3\frac{2}{8} = 3\frac{1}{4}$

A

Give the answer as a fraction.

1 $17 \div 3$ **6** $36 \div 7$

2 $47 \div 6$ **7** $29 \div 8$

3 $13 \div 2$ **8** $48 \div 5$

4 $38 \div 9$ **9** $83 \div 10$

5 $25 \div 4$ **10** $37 \div 6$

11 ⬤⬤ ⬤⬤ ⬤⬤ ⬤
      ◯◯

How many times larger is 7 than 2?

12 ⬤⬤⬤⬤⬤ ⬤⬤⬤
      ◯◯◯◯◯

How many times larger is 8 than 5?

13 ⬤⬤⬤⬤ ⬤⬤⬤⬤ ⬤
      ◯◯◯◯

How many times larger is 9 than 4?

14 ⬤⬤⬤ ⬤⬤⬤ ⬤⬤
      ◯◯◯ ◯◯◯

How many times larger is 8 than 3?

15 ⬤⬤ ⬤⬤ ⬤⬤ ⬤⬤ ⬤
      ◯◯

How many times larger is 9 than 2?

B

Give the answer as a fraction.

1 $70 \div 4$ **6** $74 \div 6$

2 $211 \div 9$ **7** $150 \div 8$

3 $103 \div 3$ **8** $165 \div 7$

4 $118 \div 7$ **9** $143 \div 4$

5 $126 \div 5$ **10** $130 \div 9$

How many times larger is:

11 1 kg than 400 g

12 £10 than £3

13 25 peas than 6 peas

14 75 cm than 20 cm

15 £36 than £5?

16 How many weeks are there in December?

17 Share 11 cakes between 4 people.

18 How many boxes holding 12 eggs are needed for:

a) 30 eggs

b) 40 eggs

c) 50 eggs?

C

Copy and complete.

1 ☐ $\div 6 = 18\frac{5}{6}$

2 ☐ $\div 9 = 26\frac{4}{9}$

3 ☐ $\div 15 = 12\frac{7}{15}$

4 ☐ $\div 8 = 21\frac{7}{8}$

5 ☐ $\div 13 = 13\frac{5}{13}$

How many times larger is:

6 £1·40 than 25p

7 1 litre than 80 ml

8 1 metre than 3 cm

9 100 beads than 6 beads

10 0·5 kg than 35 g?

11 How many 150 ml glasses can be poured from a 1 litre drink?

12 How many 60 cm lengths of string can be cut from 5 metres?

13 How many days are there in:

a) 56 hours

b) 84 hours

c) 42 hours?

I can simplify fractions by cancelling and use equivalent fractions to compare one fraction with another.

To cancel a fraction divide both numerator and denominator by the highest common factor.

Example

$\frac{12}{20} = \frac{3}{5}$ (highest common factor is 4)

To compare fractions convert them to a common denominator.

Example

Which is larger $\frac{2}{3}$ or $\frac{3}{4}$?

$\frac{2}{3} = \frac{8}{12}$ $\frac{3}{4} = \frac{9}{12}$

Answer $\frac{3}{4}$ *is larger*

A

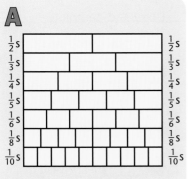

$\frac{1}{2}$s $\frac{1}{2}$s
$\frac{1}{3}$s $\frac{1}{3}$s
$\frac{1}{4}$s $\frac{1}{4}$s
$\frac{1}{5}$s $\frac{1}{5}$s
$\frac{1}{6}$s $\frac{1}{6}$s
$\frac{1}{8}$s $\frac{1}{8}$s
$\frac{1}{10}$s $\frac{1}{10}$s

Use the fraction chart to complete these equivalent fractions.

1. $\frac{1}{2} = \frac{\square}{6}$ 6. $\frac{2}{5} = \frac{\square}{10}$

2. $\frac{1}{4} = \frac{\square}{8}$ 7. $\frac{1}{3} = \frac{\square}{6}$

3. $\frac{3}{5} = \frac{\square}{10}$ 8. $\frac{3}{4} = \frac{\square}{8}$

4. $\frac{2}{3} = \frac{\square}{6}$ 9. $\frac{1}{2} = \frac{\square}{6}$

5. $\frac{1}{2} = \frac{\square}{8}$ 10. $\frac{4}{5} = \frac{\square}{10}$

Which fraction is larger?

11. $\frac{1}{2}$ or $\frac{3}{4}$ 16. $\frac{5}{8}$ or $\frac{5}{10}$

12. $\frac{2}{5}$ or $\frac{3}{10}$ 17. $\frac{1}{2}$ or $\frac{3}{5}$

13. $\frac{1}{4}$ or $\frac{3}{8}$ 18. $\frac{3}{4}$ or $\frac{5}{6}$

14. $\frac{1}{6}$ or $\frac{2}{10}$ 19. $\frac{1}{3}$ or $\frac{1}{5}$

15. $\frac{2}{3}$ or $\frac{3}{4}$ 20. $\frac{3}{5}$ or $\frac{5}{8}$

B

Cancel each fraction into its simplest form.

1. $\frac{2}{4}$ 9. $\frac{6}{9}$

2. $\frac{2}{10}$ 10. $\frac{3}{12}$

3. $\frac{4}{8}$ 11. $\frac{8}{16}$

4. $\frac{6}{10}$ 12. $\frac{70}{100}$

5. $\frac{4}{6}$ 13. $\frac{8}{12}$

6. $\frac{5}{10}$ 14. $\frac{15}{20}$

7. $\frac{6}{8}$ 15. $\frac{3}{9}$

8. $\frac{2}{6}$ 16. $\frac{6}{12}$

Write >, < or = in each box.

17. $\frac{1}{2} \square \frac{4}{10}$ 21. $\frac{4}{5} \square \frac{5}{6}$

18. $\frac{2}{3} \square \frac{4}{6}$ 22. $\frac{3}{4} \square \frac{3}{5}$

19. $\frac{2}{5} \square \frac{5}{8}$ 23. $\frac{1}{3} \square \frac{1}{6}$

20. $\frac{1}{4} \square \frac{2}{10}$ 24. $\frac{2}{5} \square \frac{4}{10}$

Find a fraction which lies between:

25. $\frac{7}{10}$ and $\frac{8}{10}$

26. $\frac{1}{4}$ and $\frac{1}{6}$

27. $\frac{4}{5}$ and $\frac{7}{8}$

28. $\frac{1}{3}$ and $\frac{2}{5}$.

C

Cancel each fraction into its lowest form.

1. $\frac{30}{100}$ 9. $\frac{14}{16}$

2. $\frac{4}{16}$ 10. $\frac{36}{60}$

3. $\frac{5}{20}$ 11. $\frac{16}{28}$

4. $\frac{6}{14}$ 12. $\frac{28}{35}$

5. $\frac{8}{40}$ 13. $\frac{9}{12}$

6. $\frac{15}{27}$ 14. $\frac{48}{100}$

7. $\frac{10}{15}$ 15. $\frac{30}{36}$

8. $\frac{90}{100}$ 16. $\frac{25}{80}$

Find the fraction which lies halfway between:

17. 1 and $\frac{1}{2}$

18. $\frac{1}{2}$ and $\frac{3}{4}$

19. $\frac{3}{10}$ and $\frac{1}{2}$

20. $\frac{1}{3}$ and $\frac{2}{3}$

21. $\frac{1}{5}$ and $\frac{2}{5}$

22. 1 and $\frac{4}{5}$

23. $\frac{1}{6}$ and $\frac{1}{2}$

24. $\frac{3}{4}$ and $\frac{5}{8}$.

I can find fractions and percentages of amounts.

Examples

$\frac{1}{8}$ of 640	$\frac{5}{8}$ of 640	10% of 40	30% of 40	5% of 40
$640 \div 8$	($\frac{1}{8}$ of 640) $\times$ 5	$\frac{1}{10}$ of 40	(10% of 40) $\times$ 3	(10% of 40) $\div$ 2
80	80×5	$40 \div 10$	4×3	$4 \div 2$
	400	4	12	2

A

Find

1. $\frac{1}{3}$ of 27
2. $\frac{1}{5}$ of 35
3. $\frac{1}{6}$ of 30
4. $\frac{1}{4}$ of 32p
5. $\frac{1}{8}$ of 48 cm

6. $\frac{3}{4}$ of 20
7. $\frac{5}{6}$ of 42
8. $\frac{2}{3}$ of 18
9. $\frac{4}{5}$ of £45
10. $\frac{2}{7}$ of 28 m

11. 10% of 70
12. 10% of 150
13. 10% of £4
14. 10% of 1 kg
15. 10% of £1·30

16. 20% of 40
17. 50% of 42
18. 30% of 250
19. 25% of 24
20. 20% of 35

B

Work out

1. $\frac{7}{9}$ of 63
2. $\frac{3}{8}$ of 48
3. $\frac{4}{7}$ of 56
4. $\frac{5}{6}$ of £1·20
5. $\frac{4}{5}$ of 80 cm
6. $\frac{3}{4}$ of 1 kg

7. 75% of 60
8. 30% of 160
9. 40% of 15
10. 30% of 400 g
11. 5% of £50
12. 90% of 150 ml

13. Ten per cent of the 130 apples in a barrel are rotten. How many can be eaten?

14. There are 150 people on a plane. One third are women. 40% are men. How many children are on the plane?

15. Thirty percent of the children in Year 6 join the Guitar Club. This is 12 children. How many children are there in Year 6?

16. A baker makes 64 cakes. 75% are sold. One quarter of the unsold cakes are eaten. How many cakes are left?

17. Forty percent of the children in 6K have milk. 18 children do not have milk. How many children are there in 6K?

C

Work out

1. $\frac{7}{8}$ of 1 litre
2. $\frac{13}{20}$ of 1 m
3. $\frac{5}{7}$ of £9·80
4. $\frac{71}{100}$ of £5·00
5. $\frac{4}{9}$ of £5·40
6. $\frac{4}{15}$ of 75p

7. 1% of 2 m
8. 75% of 3·2 km
9. 15% of 1 litre
10. 95% of 1·4 kg
11. 2·5% of £1·60
12. 40% of 19 cm

13. There are 240 pupils in a school. 45% are girls. How many boys are there in the school?

14. The 90 children in a Swimming Club are split into three groups. One sixth are Beginners. 40% are Intermediate. How many are Advanced?

15. Ian weighed 60 kg. His weight increased by 5%. What is his new weight?

16. A test was marked out of 80. Lulu had 45. Kimia had 55%. Who had the highest score and by how many marks?

17. There were 2500 people at a boy band concert. Three fifths were girls. 22% were boys. How many adults were at the concert?

I can solve problems involving direct proportion.

Examples

A glass holds 250 ml. How many glasses can be poured from a two litre bottle of lemonade?

250 ml $\times$ ☐ = 2000 ml

Answer 8 glasses

A recipe uses 0·5 kg of meat for 4 people. How much meat is needed for:

a) 1 person

b) 8 people?

Answers a) 500 g $\div$ 4 = 125 g

b) 500 g $\times$ 2 = 1 kg

A

SHORTBREAD
200 g flour
50 g caster sugar
120 g butter
Makes 8 pieces

1 Rewrite the above ingredients for:

a) 4 pieces

b) 16 pieces.

2 One dose of medicine is 10 ml. How many doses are there in a 120 ml bottle?

3 A fence panel is 2 metres wide. How many panels are needed for a fence 50 metres long?

4 One newspaper weighs 50 g. How many newspapers weigh 800 g?

5 A cyclist rides 400 metres in 1 minute. How long does it take him to cycle:

a) 2000 metres

b) 3000 metres?

B

RICE PUDDING
120 g rice
60 g caster sugar
900 ml milk
40 g butter
Serves 4

1 Rewrite the above ingredients for:

a) 1 person

b) 12 people.

2 One tile is 20 cm long. How many tiles are needed for a 4 m row?

3 How many 50 ml sherry glasses can be filled from a one litre bottle?

4 One can of beans weighs 400 g. How many cans are there in 4·8 kg?

5 Travelling at a steady speed a motorist drives 60 miles in one hour. How long will it take him to drive:

a) 150 miles

b) 200 miles?

C

RHUBARB CRUMBLE
900 g rhubarb
225 g flour
150 g butter
120 g sugar
Serves 6

1 Rewrite the above ingredients for:

a) 2 people

b) 9 people.

2 How many 40 cm lengths of ribbon can be cut from 24 metres?

3 How many 80 ml scoops of ice cream are there in a 2 litre tub?

4 One coin weighs 15 g. How many coins weigh 1·2 kg?

5 A man runs a marathon at a steady speed of 200 m per minute. How long does it take him to complete:

a) 10 km

b) 25 km

c) 42 km?

I can arrange a set of decimals in order.

Example

Arrange these decimals in ascending order.	Write in column	Put in zeros	Arrange in order
1·41, 1·4, 1·141, 1	1·41	1·410	1
	1·4	1·400	1·141
	1·141	1·141	1·4
	1	1·000	1·41

A

Copy and complete by writing < or > in the box.

1. 5·88 ☐ 8·5
2. 4·2 ☐ 4·9
3. 6·7 ☐ 6·37
4. 3·46 ☐ 4·36
5. 2·71 ☐ 1·72

6. 9·58 ☐ 9·8
7. 8·37 ☐ 8·73
8. 5·41 ☐ 5·13
9. 1·94 ☐ 4·19
10. 7·5 ☐ 7·25

Write each number shown by the arrows as a decimal fraction.

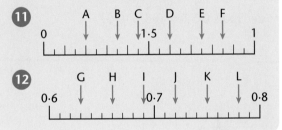

11.
12.

B

Arrange these decimals in ascending order.

1. 6·29, 0·69, 0·609, 6·09
2. 5·227, 2·257, 5·27, 2·57
3. 9·123, 9·23, 0·923, 92·3
4. 8·77, 8·272, 2·788, 2·87

Give the next five terms in each sequence.

5. 1·7, 1·6, 1·5, 1·4, 1·3
6. 0·001, 0·003, 0·005, 0·007, 0·009
7. 4·12, 4·1, 4·08, 4·06, 4·04
8. 0·065, 0·07, 0·075, 0·08, 0·085

9. Copy the line and locate the numbers.

> 1·98   1·935   1·99
> 1·965   1·915   1·95

1·9   2·0

C

Arrange these decimals in ascending order.

1. 5·656, 55·65, 5·56, 5·556, 5·66
2. 4·944, 4·99, 4·9, 4·499, 4·494
3. 0·781, 1·7, 0·187, 0·178, 0·71
4. 2·303, 0·322, 2·033, 2·32, 0·33

What number lies halfway between:

5. 2·174 and 2·178
6. 4·57 and 4·6
7. 0·32 and 0·33
8. 1·65 and 1·7
9. 3·55 and 3·85
10. 0·036 and 0·946
11. 0·25 and 1·0
12. 5·1 and 5·21?

13. Copy the line and locate the numbers.

> 1·00   0·995   1·002   1·006   0·992   1·008

0·99   1·01

I can partition numbers with up to three decimal places and give the value of each digit.

Examples

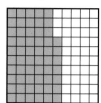

$$\frac{57}{100} = 0.57$$

Partitioned using:

- fractions $\frac{57}{100} = \frac{5}{10} + \frac{7}{100}$
- decimals $0.57 = 0.5 + 0.07$

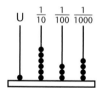

$$\frac{1634}{1000} = 1.634$$

Partitioned using:

- fractions $\frac{1634}{1000} = 1 + \frac{6}{10} + \frac{3}{100} + \frac{4}{1000}$
- decimals $1.634 = 1 + 0.6 + 0.03 + 0.004$

The value of a digit depends upon its position in a number.

Each digit in a number is 10 times higher than the digit to the right. This applies to decimal fractions as well as to whole numbers.

		T	U	·	$\frac{1}{10}$	$\frac{1}{100}$	$\frac{1}{1000}$
70	=	7	0	·	0		
7	=		7	·	0		
$\frac{7}{10}$	=		0	·	7		
$\frac{7}{100}$	=		0	·	0	7	
$\frac{7}{1000}$	=		0	·	0	0	7

A

Express the shaded part of each diagram as a fraction and as a decimal fraction.

1 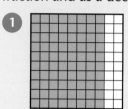   **3**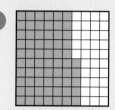

2 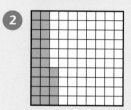   **4**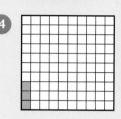

Partition each of these numbers:

a) using fractions

b) using decimals.

5 $\frac{34}{100}$ **9** $5\frac{93}{100}$ **13** $\frac{16}{100}$

6 $3\frac{29}{100}$ **10** $21\frac{9}{100}$ **14** $14\frac{4}{10}$

7 1.8 **11** 0.67 **15** 2.58

8 7.01 **12** 9.25 **16** 7.02

Give the value of the underlined figure in each of these numbers.

17 $16.\underline{8}$ **21** $0.0\underline{6}$ **25** $2.0\underline{3}$

18 $9.5\underline{2}$ **22** $3.\underline{2}9$ **26** $9.\underline{1}7$

19 $24.\underline{7}6$ **23** $58.3\underline{6}$ **27** $0.8\underline{3}1$

20 $15.\underline{4}3$ **24** $8.\underline{5}$ **28** $12.6\underline{2}$

Give the next five terms in each of these sequences.

29 $0.01, 0.03, 0.05, 0.07, 0.09$

30 $1.01, 1.02, 1.03, 1.04, 1.05$

31 $0.9, 0.92, 0.94, 0.96, 0.98$

32 $1.6, 1.65, 1.7, 1.75, 1.8$

B

Write the decimal fraction shown on each abacus.

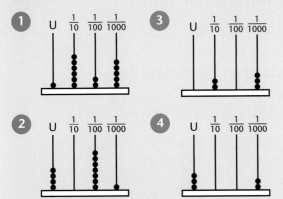

Partition using decimals.

5 $6\frac{1}{100}$ **9** $9\frac{7}{100}$ **13** $8\frac{254}{1000}$

6 $2\frac{76}{100}$ **10** $\frac{43}{1000}$ **14** $72\frac{4}{100}$

7 $\frac{397}{1000}$ **11** $1\frac{6}{1000}$ **15** $5\frac{3}{1000}$

8 $4\frac{821}{1000}$ **12** $3\frac{74}{1000}$ **16** $26\frac{26}{1000}$

Give the value of the underlined figure.

17 6.3̲4 **21** 1̲8.196 **25** 3̲6.078

18 12.8̲5 **22** 1.03̲5 **26** 4.3̲4

19 6.42̲7 **23** 0.70̲8 **27** 4.22̲2

20 1̲5.8 **24** 15.9̲2 **28** 0.5̲16

Copy and complete.

29 0.652 + 0.03 = ☐

30 2.018 + ☐ = 2.518

31 3.295 + ☐ = 3.3

32 0.476 + 0.004 = ☐

33 1.037 − 0.007 = ☐

34 2.584 − ☐ = 0.05

35 5.609 − ☐ = 0.3

36 7.246 − 0.04 = ☐

C

Write each number shown by the arrows as a decimal fraction.

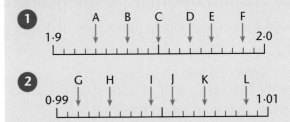

Increase the following numbers by:

$\frac{1}{10}$ $\frac{1}{100}$ $\frac{1}{1000}$

3 3 **7** 7.29 **11** 3.289

4 2.941 **8** 1.2 **12** 5

5 5.9 **9** 6 **13** 0.3

6 8.03 **10** 0.096 **14** 4.999

Give the next five terms in each of these sequences.

15 0.592, 0.593, 0.594, 0.595, 0.596

16 0.06, 0.065, 0.07, 0.075, 0.08

17 2.99, 2.992, 2.994, 2.996, 2.998

18 1.02, 1.016, 1.012, 1.008, 1.004

Copy and complete.

19 1.683 + 0.05 = ☐

20 5.134 − 0.009 = ☐

21 2.791 + 0.8 = ☐

22 1.482 − 0.6 = ☐

23 3.164 + 0.07 = ☐

24 3.261 − 0.08 = ☐

25 0.72 + ☐ = 0.743

26 1.298 − ☐ = 0.898

27 3.592 + ☐ = 3.612

28 2.793 − ☐ = 2.788

29 0.063 + ☐ = 0.123

30 9.487 − ☐ = 9.478

I can round decimals to the nearest whole number or tenth.

Always look at the column to the right of that to which you are rounding.

Examples

ROUNDING TO THE NEAREST:

WHOLE NUMBER   4·71 → 5   8·65 → 9

TENTH   2·438 → 2·4   5·85 → 5·9

APPROXIMATING CALCULATIONS

9·4 + 2·8 → 9 + 3 → 12

6·37 − 2·81 → 6·4 − 2·8 → 3·6

A

Round to the nearest whole number.

1 10·4   **7** 17·6

2 1·7   **8** 9·47

3 7·5   **9** 12·3

4 4·23   **10** 11·51

5 8·25   **11** 14·28

6 0·83   **12** 3·61

Round to the nearest pound.

13 £6·70   **19** £2·09

14 £2·40   **20** £1·37

15 £5·50   **21** £0·85

16 £12·26   **22** £3·44

17 £4·91   **23** £11·52

18 £10·73   **24** £8·65

Approximate by rounding to the nearest pound.

25 £13·80 + £5·90

26 £9·10 + £7·30

27 £26·20 + £8·60

28 £17·50 + £12·40

29 £32·40 − £16·20

30 £25·70 − £9·10

31 £40·80 − £8·50

32 £36·30 − £13·90

B

Round to the nearest:

a) whole number

b) tenth.

1 16·48   **6** 1·249

2 8·943   **7** 10·66

3 17·37   **8** 0·152

4 4·539   **9** 2·58

5 13·75   **10** 5·873

Round to the nearest:

a) pound   b) 10p.

11 £2·67   **16** £5·73

12 £0·26   **17** £0·56

13 £7·53   **18** £8·05

14 £3·85   **19** £16·34

15 £1·04   **20** £4·98

Approximate by rounding to the nearest whole number.

21 19·91 + 16·7

22 35·2 + 23·83

23 62·54 − 8·615

24 57·367 − 24·49

25 6·8 × 11

26 27·17 × 3

27 47·65 ÷ 8

28 119·91 ÷ 4

C

1 Copy the table rounding the kilograms to the nearest 100 g.

Pounds	Kilograms
1	0·454
2	0·907
3	1·361
4	1·814
5	2·268
6	2·722
7	3·175
8	3·629
9	4·082

2 Now copy the above table rounding the kilograms to the nearest 10 g.

Approximate by rounding to the nearest tenth.

3 9·45 + 3·925

4 2·13 + 6·574

5 7·262 − 0·39

6 11·78 − 4·607

7 2·461 × 4

8 5·39 × 5

9 3·482 ÷ 7

10 7·18 ÷ 9

I can mentally calculate problems involving decimals.

Example

A room is 5·8 m long and 3 m wide.

What is its area?

Use rounding to approximate answer.

Approximate answer is (6 × 3) m² or 18 m²

Actual area of room = (5·8 × 3) m²

= (5 × 3) + (0·8 × 3) m²

= (15 + 2·4) m²

= 17·4 m²

A

1 One side of a rectangle is 4·6 cm. The other side is 1·8 cm longer. What is the length of the longer side?

2 A bag contains 2·5 kg of potatoes. 0·7 kg is used. How much is left?

3 One can of fish weighs 0·3 kg. What do four cans weigh?

4 A ribbon is 3·6 metres long. It is cut in half. How long are the two ribbons?

5 A parcel weighs 1·9 kg. A second parcel weighs 1·3 kg more. What is the combined weight of the two parcels?

6 A bottle of milk holds 2 litres. 1·4 litres is drunk. How much is left?

7 A rectangular lawn is 10 metres long and 6·5 metres wide. What is its area?

B

1 Karl walks 2·3 km altogether going to and from school. How far from the school is Karl's home?

2 One egg weighs 0·06 kg. What do six eggs weigh?

3 A length of tape is 4 metres long. 2·54 metres is used. How much is left?

4 Ahmet mixes 2·4 litres of white paint and 0·75 litres of red paint. How much pink paint has he made?

5 One lolly has a capacity of 0·04 litres. What is the capacity of the four lollies in a pack?

6 A rectangular room has an area of 15 m². It is 4 m long. How wide is the room?

C

1 A bucket holds 6·3 litres of water. 1·78 litres spills out. How much water is left in the bucket?

2 One mile is 1·6 km. What is 12 miles in kilometres?

3 The total weight of four identical boxes is 6·28 kg. What does one box weigh?

4 Helena's direct route to school is 0·94 km. If she calls for her friend she walks 0·367 km further. How far is the longer route?

5 Each tube of paint used by an artist holds 0·035 litres. How much paint is there in six tubes?

6 A cake weighs 1 kg. It is cut into eight slices. What does each slice weigh?

7 Large bags of cement weigh 37·25 kg. Small bags weigh half as much. What is the weight of a small bag?

I can find the missing number in an equation and check using the inverse operation.

Examples

$0{\cdot}328 + \boxed{} = 0{\cdot}378$

The missing number is $0{\cdot}05$.

Use the inverse operation to check.

$0{\cdot}378 - 0{\cdot}05 = 0{\cdot}328$

$7{\cdot}5 \times \boxed{} = 300$

The missing number is 40.

Use the inverse operation to check.

$300 \div 40 = 7{\cdot}5$

A

Copy and complete.

1. $\boxed{} + 2{\cdot}68 = 2{\cdot}98$
2. $\boxed{} - 1{\cdot}27 = 0{\cdot}02$
3. $\boxed{} \times 4 = 2{\cdot}8$
4. $\boxed{} \div 10 = 0{\cdot}03$
5. $5{\cdot}2 + \boxed{} = 5{\cdot}24$
6. $8{\cdot}75 - \boxed{} = 8{\cdot}15$
7. $4{\cdot}3 \times \boxed{} = 43$
8. $20 \div \boxed{} = 0{\cdot}2$

Copy and complete.

9. $\boxed{} + 1{\cdot}43 = 4{\cdot}39$
10. $1{\cdot}68 + \boxed{} = 2{\cdot}57$
11. $\boxed{} - 1{\cdot}57 = 2{\cdot}24$
12. $3{\cdot}21 - \boxed{} = 1{\cdot}68$
13. $\boxed{} \times 9 = 42{\cdot}3$
14. $2{\cdot}58 \times \boxed{} = 10{\cdot}32$
15. $\boxed{} \div 6 = 0{\cdot}77$
16. $8{\cdot}7 \div \boxed{} = 2{\cdot}9$
17. Find three quarters of 26.
18. Find two fifths of 19.

B

Copy and complete.

1. $\boxed{} + 0{\cdot}07 = 3{\cdot}425$
2. $\boxed{} - 0{\cdot}003 = 1{\cdot}911$
3. $\boxed{} \times 6 = 3$
4. $\boxed{} \div 1000 = 0{\cdot}09$
5. $5{\cdot}273 + \boxed{} = 5{\cdot}873$
6. $0{\cdot}644 - \boxed{} = 0{\cdot}604$
7. $0{\cdot}732 \times \boxed{} = 73{\cdot}2$
8. $5 \div \boxed{} = 1{\cdot}25$

Use a calculator if needed.

9. $4{\cdot}35 + \boxed{} = 6{\cdot}24$
10. $\boxed{} + 1{\cdot}47 = 3{\cdot}31$
11. $8{\cdot}38 - \boxed{} = 1{\cdot}64$
12. $\boxed{} - 2{\cdot}75 = 3{\cdot}58$
13. $6{\cdot}23 \times \boxed{} = 43{\cdot}61$
14. $\boxed{} \times 9 = 22{\cdot}77$
15. $26{\cdot}08 \div \boxed{} = 3{\cdot}26$
16. $\boxed{} \div 6 = 4{\cdot}63$
17. Which number multiplied by itself gives:

    a) 1444   **b)** 4096.

C

Copy and complete.

1. $\boxed{} + 0{\cdot}14 = 0{\cdot}371$
2. $\boxed{} - 1{\cdot}005 = 2{\cdot}888$
3. $\boxed{} \times 4 = 0{\cdot}2$
4. $\boxed{} \div 5 = 0{\cdot}006$
5. $9{\cdot}217 + \boxed{} = 9{\cdot}26$
6. $0{\cdot}752 - \boxed{} = 0{\cdot}45$
7. $1{\cdot}7 \times \boxed{} = 85$
8. $48 \div \boxed{} = 0{\cdot}024$

Use a calculator.

9. $(\boxed{} \times 7) - 5{\cdot}96 = 16{\cdot}3$
10. $(\boxed{} \div 7) + 2{\cdot}16 = 4$
11. $(\boxed{} + 0{\cdot}6) \times 8 = 5$
12. $(\boxed{} - 0{\cdot}64) \div 16 = 1{\cdot}21$
13. $(\boxed{} \times 90) + 4{\cdot}9 = 13$
14. $(\boxed{} \div 24) - 0{\cdot}81 = 0{\cdot}065$
15. $(\boxed{} + 61{\cdot}1) \div 35 = 4{\cdot}92$
16. $(\boxed{} - 7{\cdot}5) \times 0{\cdot}4 = 17$
17. Find two consecutive numbers with a product of:

    a) 4556   **b)** 6972.

I can use a written method to add decimal numbers.

Example

19·56 + 6·247

19·56 rounds to 20
6·247 rounds to 6

Answer is about 26.

$$\begin{array}{r} 19\cdot56 \\ +\ 6\cdot247 \\ \hline 25\cdot807 \\ \hline {\scriptstyle 1\quad 1} \end{array}$$

Line up the decimal points.

A

Copy and complete.

1. 48·5
    +34·8

2. 3·79
    +1·84

3. 6·96
    +2·7

4. 12·5
    +5·96

5. 28·08
    +6·39

6. 9·37
    +4·48

7. 36·8
    +4·69

8. 15·68
    +7·85

9. 45·74
    +9·7

10. 87·46
    +8·54

11. Flipper ate 16·7 kg of fish. Dolly ate 3·75 kg more. How much fish did Dolly eat?

12. A triathlete swims 0·85 km, runs 5·62 km and cycles 21·35 km. How far has she travelled altogether?

B

Copy and complete.

1. 27·35
    +6·89

2. 5·786
    +3·69

3. 7·96
    +4·287

4. 6·957
    +0·743

5. 86·5
    +18·79

6. 9·837
    +1·695

7. 67·94
    +59·8

8. 79·8
    +6·53

9. 9·469
    +5·15

10. 8·73
    +0·295

11. There is 5·67 litres of water in a bucket. 0·575 litres of bleach is added. How much liquid is in the bucket?

12. Dwayne runs 400 m in 45·74 seconds. His time for the 400 m hurdles is 5·89 seconds slower. What is his 400 m hurdles time?

13. A delivery van is driven 85·35 km in the morning and 46·8 km in the afternoon. How far does it travel altogether?

C

Set out as in the example.

1. 3·756 + 84·75

2. 46·73 + 6·959

3. 51·968 + 82·74

4. 847·9 + 0·689

5. 6·059 + 57·68

6. 29·62 + 189·4

7. 5·834 + 38·76

8. 474·9 + 5·631

9. 36·569 + 28·07

10. 437·58 + 8·972

11. In one year London had 28·72 inches of rainfall and Glasgow had 16·489 inches more. What was Glasgow's rainfall?

12. A safe weighs 192·88 kg. The gold inside it weighs 268·45 kg. What is the combined weight of the safe and the gold?

I can use a written method to subtract decimal numbers.

Examples   COUNTING UP   DECOMPOSITION

2·427 − 0·683

Estimate

2·4 − 0·7 = 1·7

Answer is about 1·7

COUNTING UP

$$
\begin{array}{r}
2{\cdot}427 \\
-0{\cdot}683 \\
\hline
0{\cdot}017 \rightarrow 0{\cdot}7 \\
0{\cdot}3 \;\;\rightarrow 1{\cdot}0 \\
1{\cdot}427 \rightarrow 2{\cdot}427 \\
\hline
1{\cdot}744 \\
\hline
{\scriptstyle 1}
\end{array}
$$

DECOMPOSITION

$$
\begin{array}{r}
{}^{1}\;\;{}^{13}\;{}^{1} \\
\cancel{2}\cdot\cancel{4}\,2\,7 \\
-0\cdot6\,8\,3 \\
\hline
1\cdot7\,4\,4
\end{array}
$$

2·5 − 1·73

$$
\begin{array}{r}
{}^{1}\;\;{}^{14}\;{}^{1} \\
\cancel{2}\cdot\cancel{5}\,0 \\
-1\cdot7\,3 \\
\hline
0\cdot7\,7
\end{array}
$$
Put in the missing zero.

A

Copy and complete.

1. 37·4
    −16·8

2. 48·5
    −23·7

3. 60·9
    −34·5

4. 73·7
    −29·3

5. 59·2
    −48·6

6. 7·35
    −5·88

7. 6·38
    −2·76

8. 4·80
    −1·37

9. 3·94
    −1·67

10. 9·23
    −4·56

11. When she was born Lily weighed 3·69 kg. Five months later she weighed 6·25 kg. How much had her weight increased?

B

Copy and complete.

1. 4·16
    −2·39

2. 35·1
    −29·3

3. 5·32
    −2·85

4. 82·6
    −38·9

5. 3·51
    −2·93

6. 0·583
    −0·256

7. 3·390
    −2·618

8. 1·416
    −0·273

9. 8·675
    −3·279

10. 7·350
    −6·974

11. A rope is 6·35 metres long. 2·79 metres is cut off. How long is the rope that is left?

12. A parcel weighs 1·255 kg. A second parcel weighs 0·672 kg less. What is the weight of the lighter parcel?

13. A jug holds 3·75 litres of orange. 1·275 litres is drunk. How much is left?

C

Set out as in the examples.

1. 14·32 − 6·5

2. 3·21 − 0·526

3. 4·319 − 2·74

4. 8·13 − 1·642

5. 27·4 − 9·65

6. 3·625 − 0·79

7. 80·2 − 13·75

8. 5·82 − 2·458

9. 36·5 − 1·79

10. 9·42 − 0·785

11. A bath holds 64·38 litres of water. 0·725 litres evaporates. How much water is now in the bath?

12. Casey weighs 42·1 kg. Tanya is 3·54 kg lighter. What does Tanya weigh?

13. A racing car completes its first lap in 91·4 seconds. Its second lap is 2·66 seconds faster. How long does the second lap take?

I can solve multi-step word problems.

Example

A bike costs £139. In a sale the price is reduced by 20%. What does the bike cost in the sale?

$20\% = \frac{1}{5}$

£139 ÷ 5 = £27·80

£139 − £27·80 = £111·20

The sale price is £111·20

A

1. A ball of string is 15 m long. 4·3 m is cut off. A further 1·25 m is cut off. How much string is left?

2. A box holding 10 cans weighs 3·8 kg. The box weighs 0·2 kg. How much does each can weigh?

3. A greengrocer has seven boxes each containing 40 red apples. He also has five boxes of green apples. There are 400 apples altogether. How many green apples are there in each box?

4. Hazel buys three cards and a book for £5·34. The cards cost 45p each. How much does the book cost?

5. At 6 pm the temperature is 2°C. By midnight it has fallen 5°C. Between midnight and 6 am it rises 2°C. What is the temperature at 6 am?

B

1. Gill has 1·2 kg of flour. She uses 0·45 kg to make bread and 0·28 kg for pastry. How much flour does she have left?

2. Aaron buys four drinks at 65p each and two sandwiches at £1·35 each. How much change will he receive from £10?

3. The perimeter of a room is 21·2 metres. One wall is 4·6 m long. What is the area of the floor?

4. The temperature in London is 3°C. In Leeds it is 4° colder. In Scotland it is 3° colder than in Leeds. What is the temperature in Scotland?

5. How many minutes are there in two weeks?

C

1. A carpet costs £24 per square metre. How much will it cost to carpet a room 5 m long and 3·86 m wide?

2. Ashley won a race in 57·92 seconds. Adam was 1·48 seconds slower and Robert was 0·69 seconds behind Adam. What was Robert's time?

3. In one year in Siberia the highest temperature was 26°C and the lowest was −42°C. In London the highest temperature was 33°C and the range of temperature was one half of that in Siberia. What was the lowest temperature in London?

4. Small cans weigh 0·375 kg. Large cans weigh 0·725 kg. What is the total weight of four small and three large cans?

5. Cheese costs £4·20 for 1 kg. What does 350 g cost?

I can use my knowledge of multiplication facts to derive related facts.

A
Write the answers only.

1. 0.6×3
2. 0.5×8
3. 0.6×4
4. 0.2×9

5. 0.6×2
6. 0.3×6
7. 0.8×5
8. 0.5×7

9. 0.3×4
10. 0.8×9
11. 0.6×8
12. 0.9×2

13. 0.2×7
14. 0.6×5
15. 0.8×3
16. 0.7×6

17. $1.2 \div 6$
18. $2.8 \div 7$
19. $1.4 \div 2$
20. $4.5 \div 9$

21. $2.0 \div 5$
22. $5.6 \div 8$
23. $2.7 \div 3$
24. $2.0 \div 4$

25. $4.9 \div 7$
26. $2.5 \div 5$
27. $2.4 \div 6$
28. $6.4 \div 8$

29. $1.5 \div 3$
30. $1.8 \div 2$
31. $2.7 \div 9$
32. $2.8 \div 4$

Use the number fact given to complete the three related facts.

33. $0.6 \times 7 = 4.2$
    $\square \times 6 = 4.2$
    $4.2 \div \square = \square$
    $4.2 \div \square = \square$

34. $5 \times 0.9 = 4.5$
    $\square \times \square = 4.5$
    $4.5 \div \square = \square$
    $4.5 \div \square = \square$

B
Copy and complete.

1. $0.7 \times \square = 1.4$
2. $0.9 \times \square = 7.2$
3. $0.08 \times \square = 0.32$
4. $0.06 \times \square = 0.36$

5. $\square \times 4 = 3.6$
6. $\square \times 7 = 2.1$
7. $\square \times 8 = 0.56$
8. $\square \times 7 = 0.35$

9. $1.8 \div \square = 0.6$
10. $6.3 \div \square = 0.7$
11. $0.16 \div \square = 0.08$
12. $0.3 \div \square = 0.05$

13. $\square \div 7 = 0.9$
14. $\square \div 5 = 0.8$
15. $\square \div 8 = 0.06$
16. $\square \div 4 = 0.09$

Use the number fact given to complete the three related facts.

17. $3.78 \div 1.4 = 2.7$
    $3.78 \div \square = \square$
    $1.4 \times \square = \square$
    $2.7 \times \square = \square$

18. $0.3 \times 6 = 1.8$
    $0.06 \times \square = 0.18$
    $0.03 \times \square = 0.018$
    $1.8 \div \square = 0.06$

C
Copy and complete.

1. $0.07 \times \square = 0.56$
2. $0.006 \times \square = 0.012$
3. $0.9 \times \square = 0.54$
4. $0.03 \times \square = 0.021$

5. $\square \times 5 = 0.02$
6. $\square \times 9 = 0.54$
7. $\square \times 0.4 = 0.2$
8. $\square \times 0.8 = 0.064$

9. $0.45 \div \square = 0.09$
10. $0.042 \div \square = 0.007$
11. $0.24 \div \square = 0.003$
12. $4.2 \div \square = 0.06$

13. $\square \div 9 = 0.009$
14. $\square \div 4 = 0.07$
15. $\square \div 0.8 = 0.5$
16. $\square \div 0.5 = 0.06$

Use the number fact given to complete the four related facts.

17. $23 \times 39 = 897$
    $2.3 \times 3.9 = \square$
    $0.39 \times \square = 0.897$
    $8.97 \div \square = 0.39$
    $0.897 \div \square = 0.023$

18. $7 \times 8 = 56$
    Use the above fact to write a family of facts involving decimals.

I can multiply and divide decimals to solve word problems.

Example

One inch is 2·5 cm.
A banana is 7·8 inches long.
What is its length in
centimetres?

Approximate first
7·8 rounds to 8
2 × 8 = 16
3 × 8 = 24
16 < Answer < 24

$$\begin{array}{r} 78 \\ \times\ 25 \\ \hline 1560 \\ 390 \\ \hline 1950 \end{array}$$

Answer = 19·5 cm

A

1. One can of beans weighs 0·4 kg. What do 16 cans weigh?

2. A square field has a perimeter of 3·16 km. How long is each side?

3. At midday a shadow is 0·45 m long. At 6 p.m. it is eight times longer. How long is the shadow at 6 p.m.?

4. Forty bars of chocolate weigh 9·6 kg. What does one bar weigh?

5. How many 0·5 litre bottles can be filled from 10 litres of water?

6. How many 0·7 litre bottles can be filled from 8·4 litres of wine?

B

1. One gallon is 4·55 litres. A car's petrol tank holds 7 gallons. What is the tank's capacity in litres?

2. One lap of a running track is 0·4 km. How many laps are there in a 10 km race?

3. One pound is worth 1·4 Euros.
   a) How many Euros is £6·40?
   b) How many pounds is 49 Euros?

4. How many 0·2 litre cartons can be filled from 4 milk churns each holding 12·5 litres?

5. One kilometre is 0·62 miles.
   a) What is 25 km in miles?
   b) What is 27·9 miles in kilometres?

6. One hundred and fifty Oxo cubes weigh 0·9 kg. What does one Oxo cube weigh?

C

1. The average width of Simon's books is 1·6 cm. How many metres of shelving does he need to store his 275 books?

2. One lolly has a capacity of 0·065 litres. How many lollies can be made from 8·32 litres of the liquid mixture?

3. One kilogram is 2·2 lb. A sack contains 51·7 lb of potatoes. What do the potatoes weigh in kilograms?

4. A roll of kitchen towels is 9·68 m long. Each towel is 22 cm long. How many towels are there in each roll?

5. A room is 5·4 m long and 3·8 m wide. How much will it cost to carpet the room:
   a) at £17·50 per square metre
   b) at £9·30 per square metre?

I can use symbols to write a formula.

Examples

Write a formula for:

① the number of days (*d*) in *w* weeks
Answer *d* = 7*w*

② the *n*th term of this sequence
1 3 5 7 9
*n*th term = 2*n* − 1

③ the perimeter (*p*) of this rectangle.
Answer *p* = 2*a* + 2*b*

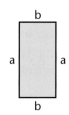

A

Write a formula for the perimeter (*p*) of each shape.

①
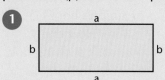
a *b* *b* *a*

②
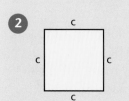
c *c* *c* *c*

③

d *f* *e*

④
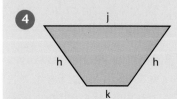
j *h* *h* *k*

⑤
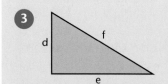
ℓ *ℓ* *ℓ* *ℓ* *ℓ* *ℓ*

⑥
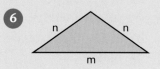
n *n* *m*

B

Write a formula for the number of

① glasses *g* in *y* bottles if one bottle holds 8 glasses

② fish *f* needed to feed *s* seals if each seal eats 6 fish

③ wheels *w* on *b* bicycles

④ months *m* in *y* years

⑤ minutes *m* in *h* hours

⑥ legs *ℓ* on *s* spiders and *a* ants

⑦ sides *s* in *p* pentagons

⑧ vertices *v* in *h* hexagonal prisms.

Find the cost of:

⑨ 10 pens at *x* pence each

⑩ *y* sweets at 20 pence each

⑪ 4 books at £*x* each

⑫ *d* dollars at £0·6 each.

C

Draw and label the shape whose perimeter is given by each formula.

① a triangle
p = 3*a*

② an irregular pentagon
p = 3*a* + 2*c*

③ a quadrilateral
p = 3*d* + *e*

④ an irregular hexagon
p = 3*f* + 2*g* + *h*

Write a formula for the *n*th term of each sequence.

⑤ 2, 4, 6, 8, 10

⑥ 3, 6, 9, 12, 15

⑦ −3, −2, −1, 0, 1

⑧ 1, 4, 9, 16, 25

⑨ 3, 5, 7, 9, 11

⑩ 2, 5, 8, 11, 14

⑪ A car has *x* litres of petrol in its tank. One half is used on Monday. A further 2 litres on Tuesday. How much petrol is left?

I can use a calculator to solve number problems, using rounding to approximate an answer as a check.

Example

$0.63 \times \boxed{} = 2.961$

Using a calculator
$2.961 \div 0.63 = 4.7$

2.961 rounds to 3
0.63 rounds to 0.6
$3 \div 0.6 = 5$
Answer is approximately 5

A

For each of the following:

a) copy and complete by putting a decimal point in the answer

b) use a calculator to check.

1. $264.8 - 185.15 = 7965$
2. $6.29 - 0.543 = 5747$
3. $132.7 + 12.98 = 14568$
4. $0.185 + 0.647 = 832$

5. $5.76 \times 6.45 = 37152$
6. $239 \times 5.3 = 12667$
7. $0.48 \times 379 = 18192$
8. $39.4 \times 7.37 = 290378$

Use a calculator.
Copy and complete.

9. $2.97 + \boxed{} = 5.32$
10. $4.49 + \boxed{} = 5.16$
11. $\boxed{} - 3.75 = 0.68$
12. $\boxed{} - 1.83 = 6.47$

13. $69 \times \boxed{} = 296.7$
14. $35.5 \times \boxed{} = 198.8$
15. $2195.2 \div \boxed{} = 34.3$
16. $27.257 \div \boxed{} = 5.62$

B

For each of the following:

a) use rounding to choose the approximate answer

b) use a calculator to find the correct answer.

1. 7.3×6.9
   490   49   4.9   0.49

2. 0.38×5.4
   200   20   2   0.2

3. 8.4×2.7
   240   24   2.4   0.24

4. 0.65×0.42
   28   2.8   0.28   0.028

Use a calculator.
Copy and complete.

5. $64 \times \boxed{} = 20.48$
6. $0.4 \times \boxed{} = 154.8$
7. $0.864 \div \boxed{} = 1.92$
8. $202.92 \div \boxed{} = 3.8$

9. $6\boxed{} \times \boxed{}4 = 5628$
10. $12\boxed{} \times \boxed{}9 = 4914$
11. $19\,437 \div 34\boxed{} = \boxed{}7$
12. $12\,255 \div \boxed{}3 = 28\boxed{}$

C

For each of the following:

a) copy and complete by putting the decimal point in the answer

b) use a calculator to check.

1. $126.9 \times 7.1 = 90099$
2. $255 \times 28.8 = 73440$
3. $0.92 \times 6.3 = 5796$
4. $31.64 \times 72.5 = 22939$
5. $0.815 \times 61.8 = 50367$
6. $3.45 \times 79.6 = 27462$

One pound = 1.46 Euros

7. Change £5125 to Euros.
8. Change €369.6 to pounds.

1 lb = 0.454 kg

9. Change 35 lb to kilograms.
10. Change 215.65 kg to pounds.

One gallon = 0.22 litres

11. Change 78 litres to gallons.
12. Change 630.3 gallons to litres.

I can work out the squares of multiples of 10.

Example

When a number is multiplied by itself you get a square number.
They are called square numbers because they make square patterns.

$1^2 = 1 \times 1 = 1$ $2^2 = 2 \times 2 = 4$ $3^2 = 3 \times 3 = 9$ $4^2 = 4 \times 4 = 16$

A

Work out

1 6^2 5 2^2

2 3^2 6 9^2

3 5^2 7 4^2

4 10^2 8 7^2

Which number when
multiplied by itself gives:

9 16   13 64

10 49   14 100

11 4   15 25

12 36   16 81?

Copy and complete.

17 $20^2 = 20 \times 20$

   $= 20 \times \square \times 10$

   $= \square \times 10$

   $= \square$

18 $50^2 = 50 \times \square$

   $= 50 \times \square \times \square$

   $= \square \times \square$

   $= \square$

19 $30^2 = \square \times 30$

   $= \square \times 3 \times \square$

   $= \square \times \square$

   $= \square$

B

Work out

1 40^2 5 70^2

2 80^2 6 100^2

3 50^2 7 60^2

4 20^2 8 90^2

Which number when
multiplied by itself gives:

9 900   13 3600

10 4900   14 6400

11 1600   15 2500

12 10 000   16 8100?

$2^2 = 1^2 + 1 + 2 = 5$
$3^2 = 2^2 + 2 + 3 = 9$
$4^2 = 3^2 + 3 + 4 = 16$

17 Copy the above
    pattern and continue it
    to the line for 12^2.

Use the pattern to work
out:

18 31^2 22 19^2

19 91^2 23 49^2

20 101^2 24 79^2

21 61^2 25 39^2.

C

Work out

1 200^2 7 $80^2 - 30^2$

2 500^2 8 $60^2 + 20^2$

3 900^2 9 $100^2 - 70^2$

4 400^2 10 $50^2 + 100^2$

5 1000^2 11 $60^2 - 40^2$

6 700^2 12 $30^2 + 90^2$

Lagrange's Theorem

*Every whole number can be
written as the sum of four or
fewer square numbers.*

Examples

$19 = 16 + 1 + 1 + 1$
$35 = 25 + 9 + 1$

Make the following
numbers from four or fewer
square numbers.

13 15   19 438

14 24   20 16 400

15 62   21 14 500

16 115   22 2436

17 168   23 6190

18 140   24 9909

I can find the prime factors of two-digit numbers.

Factors are numbers that divide exactly into another number.

A prime number is a number which is only divisible by itself and by one.

A factor which is also a prime number is a prime factor.

To find the prime factors of a number we can use a factor tree.

Prime factors can be used to find products.

A factor tree for 63

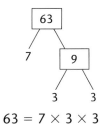

$63 = 7 \times 3 \times 3$

A factor tree for 36

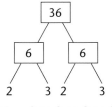

$36 = 2 \times 3 \times 2 \times 3$

Example
$42 \times 36 = 42 \times 3 \times 2 \times 2 \times 3 = 126 \times 2 \times 2 \times 3 = 252 \times 2 \times 3 = 756 \times 2 = 1512$

A

Find all the factors of:

1. 6
2. 16
3. 20
4. 22
5. 27
6. 30
7. 32
8. 36.

Find all the prime numbers between:

9. 10 and 20
10. 20 and 30
11. 30 and 40
12. 40 and 50.

Write down the next prime number after:

13. 74
14. 62
15. 90
16. 48
17. 84
18. 69
19. 55
20. 100.

B

Use a factor tree to find all the prime factors of:

1. 24
2. 40
3. 42
4. 54
5. 72
6. 75
7. 88
8. 90.

Find a pair of prime numbers which give a total of:

9. 19
10. 22
11. 63
12. 44.

13. Find six pairs of prime numbers which give a total of 100.

Explain why these numbers are not prime numbers.

14. 87
15. 91
16. 146
17. 2001
18. 135
19. 143

C

Use a factor tree to find all the prime factors of:

1. 48
2. 60
3. 81
4. 84
5. 100
6. 144
7. 162
8. 256.

Break the second number down into prime factors to help work out:

9. 37×12
10. 38×25
11. 61×48
12. 53×42
13. 56×45
14. 65×56
15. 76×64
16. 89×72.

Explain why these numbers are not prime numbers.

17. 161
18. 209
19. 2457
20. 187
21. 377
22. 5001

I can identify the patterns made by multiples of numbers in a 100 square and in grids of different sizes.

Look at the 100 square.

The multiples of 2 make vertical lines.

The multiples of 3 make diagonal lines going down to the left.

The multiples of 4 make a knight's move pattern. (1 down and 2 across)

Some examples of the above patterns are shown. The patterns are repeated throughout the grid.

1	2	3	4	5	6	7	8	9	10
11	12	13	14	15	16	17	18	19	20
21	22	23	24	25	26	27	28	29	30
31	32	33	34	35	36	37	38	39	40
41	42	43	44	45	46	47	48	49	50
51	52	53	54	55	56	57	58	59	60
61	62	63	64	65	66	67	68	69	70
71	72	73	74	75	76	77	78	79	80
81	82	83	84	85	86	87	88	89	90
91	92	93	94	95	96	97	98	99	100

A

Look at a 100 square.

1 How many vertical lines are made up from multiples of 2?

2 How many diagonal lines are made up from multiples of 3?

What pattern is made by the multiples of:

3 5   **5** 8   **7** 10   **9** 12

4 6   **6** 9   **8** 11   **10** 4?

Look at the nine-column grid.

This time the pattern made by the multiples of 2 makes a chessboard pattern.

What is the pattern made by the multiples of:

11 3   **14** 7   **17** 10

12 4   **15** 8   **18** 11

13 5   **16** 9   **19** 2?

1	2	3	4	5	6	7	8	9
10	11	12	13	14	15	16	17	18
19	20	21	22	23	24	25	26	27
28	29	30	31	32	33	34	35	36
37	38	39	40	41	42	43	44	45
46	47	48	49	50	51	52	53	54
55	56	57	58	59	60	61	62	63
64	65	66	67	68	69	70	71	72
73	74	75	76	77	78	79	80	81

Look at the eight-column grid.

What is the pattern made by the multiples of:

1 2   **4** 5   **7** 8

2 3   **5** 6   **8** 9

3 4   **6** 7   **9** 10?

Predict what the pattern would be for the multiples of these numbers in a seven-column grid.

10 2   **12** 4   **14** 6   **16** 8

11 3   **13** 5   **15** 7   **17** 9

18 Write out the first five rows of a seven-column grid.
Were your predictions correct?

1	2	3	4	5	6	7	8
9	10	11	12	13	14	15	16
17	18	19	20	21	22	23	24
25	26	27	28	29	30	31	32
33	34	35	36	37	38	39	40
41	42	43	44	45	46	47	48
49	50	51	52	53	54	55	56
57	58	59	60	61	62	63	64

C

1 Copy and complete this table showing the patterns of multiples in different size grids.

NO. OF COLUMNS	MULTIPLES OF								
	2	3	4	5	6	7	8	9	10
10	V	Dl	K	V	Kr	O			
9	C	V							
8									
7									X
6								X	X
5							X	X	X
4						X	X	X	X
3					X	X	X	X	X

KEY
V – vertical
Dl – diagonal (left)
Dr – diagonal (right)
Kl – knight's move (left)
Kr – knight's move (right)
K – knight's move (left and right)
C – chessboard
O – none of the above

2 Use your table to predict the pattern made by the multiples of the numbers from 2 to 11 in:
a) an eleven-column grid
b) a twelve-column grid.

I can find the rule for a number sequence.

To find the rule look at the differences between the terms.

Examples

4	0	−4	−8	−12	The rule is *subtract 4.*
3	6	12	24	48	The rule is *multiply by 2.*
1	3	6	10	15	The rule is *add one more each time.*

A

Write the first six numbers in each sequence.

	Start at	Rule
1	62	−3
2	2	$+\frac{1}{2}$
3	1·5	−0·25
4	−100	+50
5	7	−2
6	47	+9

Complete each sequence

7 1 ☐ ☐ 2·5 3 3·5

8 −10 −6 −2 ☐ ☐

9 ☐ ☐ 12 20 30 42

10 $\frac{1}{4}$ $\frac{1}{2}$ ☐ ☐ $1\frac{1}{4}$

11 ☐ 901 802 703 ☐

12 67 ☐ 45 ☐ 23

2   4   6   8   10   12

Look at the above pattern. Write down:

13 the 7th term

14 the 10th term

15 the 25th term

16 a rule for the *n*th term.

B

Complete each sequence.

1 ☐ ☐ 1 3 5 7

2 ☐ ☐ 1·1 1·3 1·5

3 $\frac{1}{4}$ ☐ $1\frac{1}{4}$ ☐ $2\frac{1}{4}$

4 2 4 7 ☐ ☐ 22

5 ☐ 42 63 ☐ 105

6 −33 −23 −13 ☐ ☐

4   8   12   16   20

Look at the above pattern. Write down:

7 the 9th term

8 the 15th term

9 the 100th term

10 a formula for the *n*th term.

*n*th term = ☐

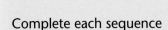

Look at the pattern of beads. What colour is:

11 the 20th bead

12 the 35th bead

13 the 50th bead

14 the 100th bead?

C

Copy each sequence and write the next three numbers.

1 1·5 2·0 3·0 4·5

2 100 82 64 46

3 10 7 4 1

4 $2\frac{1}{2}$ $2\frac{1}{8}$ $1\frac{3}{4}$ $1\frac{3}{8}$

5 12·4 9·9 7·4 4·9

6 0·1 0·2 0·4 0·8

Write down a formula for the *n*th term of each pattern.

7 7 14 21 28 35

8 3 5 7 9 11

9 1 4 9 16 25

10 −2 −4 −6 −8 −10

Look at the pattern of beads. What colour is:

11 the 20th bead

12 the 50th bead

13 the 70th bead

14 the 100th bead?

I can explain the relationship between the number of lines of symmetry of a shape and the angle between those lines.

A

1 How many lines of symmetry does each shape have?

    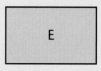 

2 Copy the shapes and draw on the lines of symmetry.

3 Which shapes have lines of symmetry which meet at 90°?

4 Which shape has lines of symmetry which meet at:
   a) 60°   b) 45°   c) 30°?

B

Copy and complete this table showing the angle between the lines of symmetry of regular polygons.

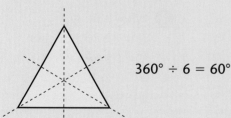

360° ÷ 6 = 60°

SHAPE	LINES OF SYMMETRY	ANGLE
equilateral triangle	3	60°
square		
regular pentagon		
regular hexagon		
regular octagon		
regular decagon		

C

1 a) Draw 6 spokes of equal length with a 60° angle between them.

   b) Join up the ends of the spokes to make a regular hexagon.

   a)   b)

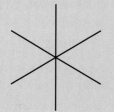   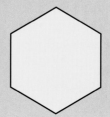

2 Use this method to draw:
   a) a square
   b) a regular pentagon
   c) a regular octagon.

3 Use this method to copy these shapes.

I can describe the properties of different quadrilaterals.

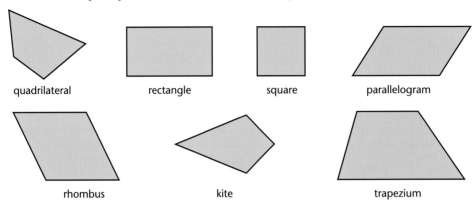

quadrilateral   rectangle   square   parallelogram

rhombus   kite   trapezium

A

1. What is the name for a regular quadrilateral?

2. Write down the names of four quadrilaterals which:

   a) are symmetrical

   b) have 2 pairs of parallel sides.

3. Write down the names of two quadrilaterals which:

   a) have 4 right angles

   b) have 4 equal sides

   c) have 2 pairs of equal opposite sides.

4. Write down the name of a quadrilateral which:

   a) has one pair of parallel sides only

   b) has 2 pairs of equal adjacent (next to each other) sides.

5. Sketch the four symmetrical quadrilaterals and draw on all the lines of symmetry.

B

1. Use squared paper. Draw the following quadrilaterals using the intersections of the squares.

   a) a rhombus

   b) a parallelogram

   c) a kite

   d) a symmetrical trapezium

   Example

   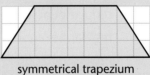

   symmetrical trapezium

2. Measure the angles of each shape. Show pairs of equal angles.

3. Draw on the diagonals of each shape. Which shapes have diagonals which:

   a) are of equal length

   b) cut each other in half

   c) are perpendicular?

4. Investigate the diagonals of a square and a rectangle.

C

1.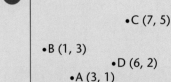

   •C (7, 5)

   •B (1, 3)
   •D (6, 2)
   •A (3, 1)

   Draw the quadrilateral ABCD on a grid. Label the shape.

2. What type of quadrilateral do you make if you move:

   a) A to (0, 0)

   b) B to (4, 4)

   c) C to (3, 5)

   d) D to (5, 7)

   e) A to (2, 6)?

3. Draw the five quadrilaterals and check your predictions.

4. Find the sum of the angles of each quadrilateral. What do you notice?

5. Draw some different types of quadrilaterals. Find the sum of the angles of each shape.

I can convert between units of measurement.

UNITS OF LENGTH

km —×1000→ m —×100→ cm —×10→ mm

km ←÷1000— m ←÷100— cm ←÷10— mm

UNITS OF MASS

kg —×1000→ g

kg ←÷1000— g

UNITS OF CAPACITY

litres —×1000→ ml

litres ←÷1000— ml

A

Copy and complete.

1. 32 mm = ☐ cm
2. 76 mm = ☐ cm
3. 8·1 cm = ☐ mm
4. 2·5 cm = ☐ mm

5. 580 cm = ☐ m
6. 190 cm = ☐ m
7. 0·3 m = ☐ cm
8. 4·2 m = ☐ cm

9. 6700 m = ☐ km
10. 5500 m = ☐ km
11. 3·8 km = ☐ m
12. 2·4 km = ☐ m

Which metric unit would you use to measure:

13. the length of a swimming pool
14. the weight of a slice of bread
15. the capacity of a can of cola
16. the width of a pencil?

B

Copy and complete.

1. 286 cm = ☐ m
2. 639 cm = ☐ m
3. 0·63 m = ☐ cm
4. 9·07 m = ☐ cm

5. 3150 m = ☐ km
6. 7240 m = ☐ km
7. 2·58 km = ☐ m
8. 4·91 km = ☐ m

9. 1180 g = ☐ kg
10. 8070 g = ☐ kg
11. 6·52 kg = ☐ g
12. 5·73 kg = ☐ g

Which metric unit would you use to measure:

13. the weight of a sack of garden compost
14. the capacity of a sack of garden compost
15. the perimeter of a book
16. the border of a country?

C

Copy and complete.

1. 1272 m = ☐ km
2. 6618 m = ☐ km
3. 3·905 km = ☐ m
4. 8·586 km = ☐ m

5. 5124 g = ☐ kg
6. 2851 g = ☐ kg
7. 0·363 kg = ☐ g
8. 9·043 kg = ☐ g

9. 4715 ml = ☐ litres
10. 9397 ml = ☐ litres
11. 0·139 litres = ☐ ml
12. 4·145 litres = ☐ ml

Copy and complete by choosing the best estimate.

13. A chair leg has a length of (0·003 m, 0·03 m, 0·3 m).
14. A car has a weight of (10 000 g, 100 000 g, 1 000 000 g).
15. A cereal bowl has a capacity of (0·045 ℓ, 0·45 ℓ, 4·5 ℓ).
16. A running track is (0·001 km, 0·01 km, 0·1 km) long.

I can use frequency tables and draw and interpret bar charts with grouped data.

If the spread of a set of data is too large it is usually necessary to group the data before displaying it in the form of a graph.

Example
The ages of Mrs. Evan's family on the occasion of her 100th birthday party.

78	18	1	35	26	9
54	32	45	15	11	59
39	42	0	33	21	74
6	28	48	7	24	12
100	57	37	3	81	60

A tally chart showing the grouped ages.

Age	Tally	Frequency
0–19	ℍℍ ℍℍ	10
20–39	ℍℍ ℍℍ	9
40–59	ℍℍ ℍ	6
69–79	ℍℍℍ	3
80–99	ℍ	1
100+	ℍ	1
Total		30

The data in the tally chart can be displayed in a graph.

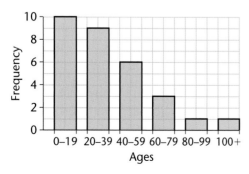

A

1 This bar chart shows the marks Jason achieved in his weekly spelling test.

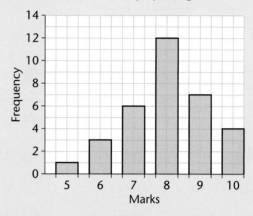

a) What was Jason's highest score?

b) What was his lowest score?

c) What was the range of his scores?

d) What was Jason's modal score?

e) How many times did Jason score 7?

f) How many times did he score less than 7?

g) How many times did he score more than 7?

h) How many times was Jason tested?

2 The portions of fruit and vegetables eaten by children in Class 6 in one day.

4	5	2	4	3	5	6	3	4	5
4	6	4	5	3	1	4	5	2	4
3	5	4	2	4	5	3	4	5	4

Make a frequency table and then display the data in a bar chart.

B

1 This bar chart shows the number of goals scored by entrants in a penalty competition.

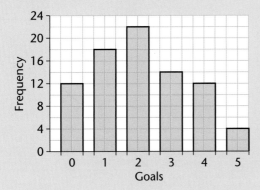

a) What was the highest number of goals scored?

b) What number of goals scored was the mode?

c) How many competitors scored more than 2 goals?

d) How many competitors scored less than 2 goals?

e) How many people took part in the competition?

f) Kelvin says
Half the competitors scored either one or two goals.
Is he right?
Explain your answer.

g) How many goals were scored altogether?

2 The lengths swum by children in Class 6 during their Sponsored Swim.

```
 6  15   1  19  23  10  12   8  11   3
12   9  14   6  12  20   1  14  17  15
 4  11  24   2  16   8  15   7  13  21
```

Group the data in sets of 5 lengths. (1–5, 6–10, etc.).

Make a tally chart and then display the data in a bar chart.

C

1 This bar chart shows the numbers of hours spent watching television in one week by the children in a Junior School.

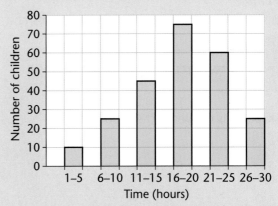

a) How many children watched television for less than 11 hours?

b) How many children watched for more than 20 hours?

c) What proportion of the children in the school watched less than 15 hours of television?

d) What proportion watched between 11 and 20 hours?

e) What proportion watched more than 20 and less than 26 hours?

f) This survey was conducted in November. Draw a graph showing how you think the hours watched would be distributed if the same survey was conducted in June.

2 The numbers of minutes spent in energetic activity by children in Year 6.

```
18  25  53  36  41  38  10  27  32  49
53  16  24  47  35  52  39  26  45  31
37  44  28  33   7  19  22  54  36  12
25  15  40  51  29  48  35  17  43  27
46  33   8  20  42  25  56  40  21  14
```

Group the data.

Make a tally chart and then display the data in a bar chart.

I can use a conversion graph.

Example

This graph converts pounds into kilograms and vice versa.

2 pounds converts to 0·9 kg to the nearest 100 g.

2 kilograms converts to 4·4 pounds.

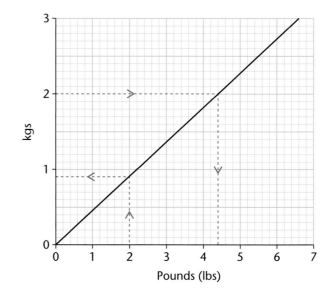

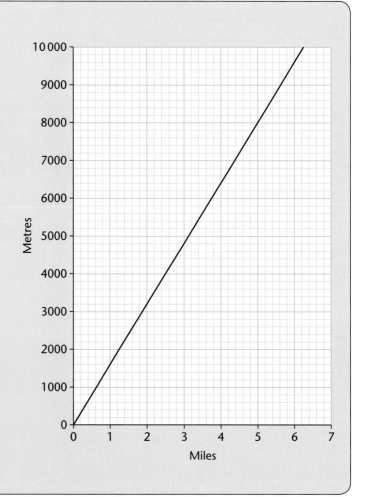

A

This graph converts metres to miles.

1 Convert to the nearest 100 m.

   a) 3 miles   **d)** 4 miles

   b) 1 mile   **e)** 5 miles

   c) 6 miles   **f)** 2 miles

2 Convert these long and middle distance running events into miles.

   a) 5000 metres

   b) 3000 m steeplechase

   c) 10 000 metres

   d) 800 metres

3 The 1500 metres is often called *the metric mile*. Which race is longer, the mile or the 1500 metres?

4 One lap of a running track is 400 m. An athlete runs 10 laps. How far has she run in miles?

B

This graph converts kilometres to miles.

1 Convert to the nearest mile.

a) 80 km   d) 152 km

b) 120 km   e) 16 km

c) 48 km   f) 136 km

2 Convert to the nearest kilometre.

a) 100 miles   d) 60 miles

b) 25 miles   e) 18 miles

c) 80 miles   f) 45 miles

3 A motorist knows his car uses one gallon of petrol for every 35 miles travelled. He drives 112 km. How much petrol has been used?

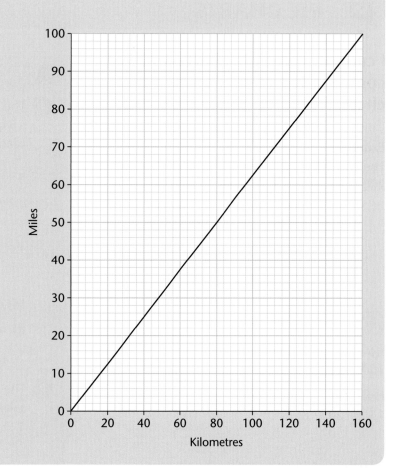

C

When your grandparents were young we measured temperatures on the Fahrenheit scale. Today, of course, we use the Celsius scale but many people still think of temperatures in degrees Fahrenheit (°F). This graph converts temperatures on one scale to the other.

1 Convert to degrees Fahrenheit.

a) 0°C   c) 15°C   e) 23°C

b) 25°C   d) −6°C   f) 5°C

2 Convert to degrees Celsius.

a) 86°F   c) 50°F   e) 68°F

b) 23°F   d) 14°F   f) 81°F

3 Which scale are people using when they talk of the temperature being:

a) on a warm day, in the 80s

b) on a cold day, below zero?

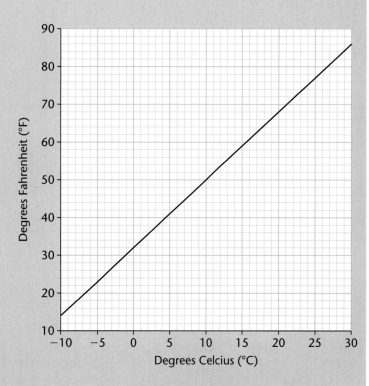

I can interpret pie charts and compare the results on two pie charts based on different totals.

Examples

The two pie charts show the favourite colours of 200 children and 120 adults.

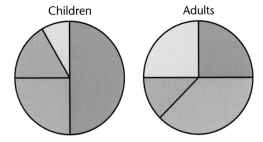

Children   Adults

How many children chose red?

100 (200 ÷ 2)

How many adults chose green?

15 (120 ÷ 8)

Did more children or adults choose blue?

Children choosing blue

$\frac{1}{4}$ of 200 = 200 ÷ 4 = 50

Adults choosing blue

$$\frac{3}{8} \text{ of } 120 = (\frac{1}{8} \text{ of } 120) \times 3$$
$$= 15 \times 3$$
$$= 45$$

Answer   *More children chose blue.*

The 300 members of the audience at a performance of Toy Story.

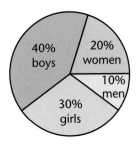

Group	Number
boys	120
girls	90
women	60
men	30

A

1 The pie chart shows the results of the 16 games played by the school netball team.

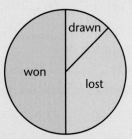

How many games were:

a) won   **b)** lost   **c)** drawn?

2 The pie chart shows the 60 people taking part in a sponsored walk.

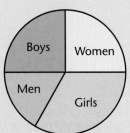

Estimate the number of walkers who were

a) boys   **b)** men   **c)** girls.

3 The pie chart shows the numbers of goals scored by a football team in 40 games.

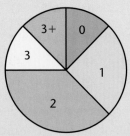

In how many games did the team score:

a) 0 goals   **b)** 1 goal   **c)** 2 goals?

B

1 The pie charts show the 36 children who belong to the Art Club and the 24 children who belong to the Dance Club.

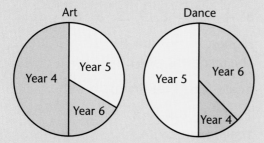

Art   Dance

a) How many Year 4 children belong to the Art Club?

b) Estimate the number of Year 6 children who belong to the Dance Club?

c) The same number of Year 5 children belong to each club. How many children?

d) How many Year 6 children belong to the Art Club?

2 The pie charts show the favourite PE activities voted for by 32 boys and 48 girls.

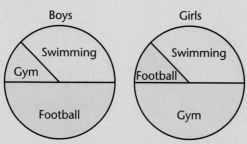

Boys   Girls

a) How many girls voted for gym?

b) Estimate how many boys voted for gym?

c) Roland says

The same number of boys and girls chose swimming.

Use both charts to explain why Roland is not right.

d) Estimate how many more boys voted for football than girls?

C

The pie charts show how 60 Year 6 pupils and 80 Year 7 pupils travel to school.

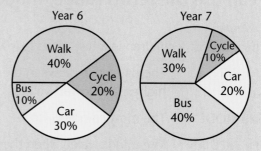

Year 6   Year 7

1 How many Year 6 children:

a) travel by bus

b) cycle?

2 How many Year 7 children:

a) cycle

b) travel by bus?

3 Lucie says

More children walk to school in Year 6 than in Year 7.

Use both charts to explain why this statement is not correct.

The pie charts show the favourite breakfast of 50 children and 40 adults.

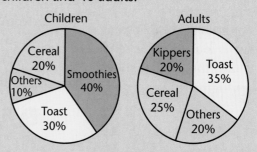

Children   Adults

4 How many children chose:

a) toast   b) smoothies?

5 How many adults chose:

a) kippers   b) toast?

6 Felicity says

The same number of both children and adults chose cereal.

Is she right? Use both charts to explain your answer.

I can use the terms range, mode, median and mean to solve problems.

Example

The marks of 9 children in a test are as follows:

8 4 7 1 8 9 3 8 6

THE RANGE — The difference between the highest and lowest values.

Highest − Lowest = 9 − 1
The range is 8 marks.

THE MODE — The most common value.

mode = 8 (three times)

THE MEDIAN — The middle value when the numbers are in size order.

1 3 4 6 ⑦ 8 8 8 9
The median is 7.

THE MEAN — The total divided by the number of items in the set.

Total marks ÷ number of children
The mean is 6. (54 ÷ 9)

A

For each group of numbers find:

a) the total   b) the mean

1. 12 5 7 4

2. 2 3 8 4 3

3. 10 17 6

4. 3 9 8 5 4 7

For each of the following sets of data find the range, mode, median and mean.

5. The ages of seven children.
   9 2 8 3 2 4 6

6. The daily hours of sunshine recorded in one week

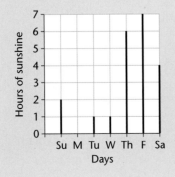

B

1. Joanne's marks in her weekly spelling test.

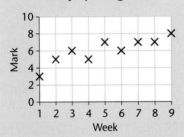

Find:

a) the range of marks
b) the modal mark
c) the median mark
d) the mean mark.

2. Tariq rolled two dice and wrote down the combined score. These are his first 10 scores.

8 6 10 5 3
7 12 6 9 5

He rolled the dice again. The mean score was now 7. What was his last score?

3. Find five numbers with a range of 12, a mode of 43 and a median of 46.

C

1. Five people work in an office. The mean age is 30 and the range of their ages is 6.
   Write each sentence below and write next to it whether it is *Possible* or *Impossible*.

a) Every person is 30 years old.

b) All the people are at least 28 years old.

c) The oldest person is 35.

d) The youngest is 24.

2. There are four classes in a school. Each class has a different number of children. One class only has 30 children. The range of class size is 5. The mean class size is 28.
   How many children are there in each of the four classes?

I can use the language of probability to describe the likelihood of an event.

The probability of an event can be placed on a scale.

| Impossible | Unlikely | Evens | Likely | Certain |

Example

① You spin a coin and get a tail.

A

Place the probabilities of these events on a scale like the one above.

1. Christmas Day will be December 25th.

2. You will learn to drive when you grow up.

3. You will have the same birthday as the Prime Minister.

4. The next child to join the school will be a girl.

5. The Queen has a cup of tea at breakfast.

6. The sun will rise in the west.

7. What is the probability that the first ball chosen will be:
   a) odd   d) under 6
   b) even   e) 3
   c) 6   f) under 3?

8. This ball is chosen. ⑤ What is the probability that the next ball chosen will be:
   a) odd   c) over 3
   b) even   d) under 3?

B

Which event is more likely? Explain why.

1. Rolling a dice and getting:
   a) a 6
   b) less than 3.

2. Drawing a card from a pack and getting:
   a) a red card
   b) a heart.

3. Spinning 2 coins and getting:
   a) 2 heads
   b) 1 head and 1 tail.

4. Nine balls numbered 1 to 9 are placed in a bag. What is the probability that the first ball chosen is:
   a) odd
   b) more than 5?

5. From the nine balls above ball ③ is chosen. What is the probability that the next ball is:
   a) odd
   b) more than 5?

6. The ① is chosen. What is the probability that the third ball is:
   a) odd
   b) more than 5?

C

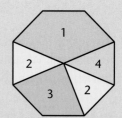

1. Using this spinner are you more likely to land on:
   a) 1 or 2
   b) 2 or 3
   c) 3 or 4
   d) an odd number or an even number?

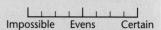
| Impossible | Evens | Certain |

2. Copy the scale. Place on the scale the probability that the above spinner will land on:
   a) 1   c) 3
   b) 2   d) 4
   e) less than 4
   f) more than 1.

3.

Which spinner is more likely to land on:
   a) an odd number
   b) an even number
   c) a number below 3
   d) a number above 3
   e) 3?

I can solve practical problems involving estimating and measurement.

Examples

100 screws weigh 450 g
What does one screw weigh?
Answer   4·5 g (450 g ÷ 100)

50 peanuts weigh 30 g.
One peanut weighs
about 0·6 g.

$$30 g ÷ 50 = (30 g ÷ 100) × 2$$
$$= 0·3 g × 2$$
$$= 0·6 g$$

A

1. A stack of 10 coins is 16 mm tall. What is the thickness of one coin?

2. Twenty sweets weigh 150 g. What is the weight of one sweet?

3. A row of 10 matches is 2·5 cm wide. What is the width of one match?

4. One hundred sheets of paper are 2 cm thick. What is the thickness of one sheet of paper?

5. In 20 minutes a cyclist travels 5 km. How far does he travel in one minute?

6. Use ten £1 coins. Estimate the width of one coin.

7. Measure how far you walk in 10 seconds. Estimate the distance you walk in one second.

8. Measure the weight of 10 identical exercise books. Estimate the weight of one book.

B

1. One hundred seeds weigh 15 g. Estimate the weight of one seed.

2. Fifty nails weigh 120 g. Estimate the weight of one nail.

3. A row of 100 staples is 5 cm long. What is the approximate width of one staple?

4. A car uses 28 litres of petrol in a 200 mile journey. Estimate how much petrol is used every mile in millilitres.

5. A car travels 1·8 km in one minute. About how far does it travel in one second in metres?

6. Estimate the weight of one pencil.

7. Collect the water from a running tap for 10 seconds. Estimate the amount of water used every second.

8. Estimate the length of time it takes you to write the letter *a*.

C

1. The 250 matches in a box weigh 50 g. What is the approximate weight of one match?

2. A stack of 40 sheets of card is 32 mm tall. What is the width of one sheet?

3. A plane flies 540 km in one hour. Estimate its average speed in metres per second.

4. In one day a dripping tap loses 36 litres of water. Approximately how much water is lost each minute?

5. Hugo runs 270 m in one minute. About how far does he run every second?

6. Estimate the thickness of the sheets of paper in your reading book. (Note that one sheet is 2 pages.)

7. Estimate the weight of one sheet of A4 paper.

8. Estimate the length of time it takes you to read one word.

I can solve word problems involving measures, converting between units where necessary.

Example

How many 80 ml scoops of ice cream are there in a 4 litre tub?

4 litres = 4000 ml
4000 ÷ 80 = 50
There are fifty 80 ml scoops in a 4 litre tub.

A

1. A test tube holds 0·1 litres of liquid. 38 ml is added. How much liquid is there in the tube now?

2. The total weight of eight apples is 1·2 kg. What is the mean weight of the apples?

3. How many 250 ml glasses can be filled from three litres of juice?

4. How many 40 cm lengths can be cut from a 3·6 m plank?

5. A box of 50 chocolate bars weighs 6·5 kg. What does each bar weigh?

6. A mountain peak is 4·26 km above sea level. A climber is 549 m below the summit. How high is the climber?

B

1. A loaf of bread weighs 1 kg. It contains 25 slices. What does each slice weigh in grams?

2. A rectangular field is 1·586 km long and 234 m wide. What is its perimeter?

3. One pound equals 1·4 Euros. Phoebe has 70 Euros. How much is this in pounds?

4. The cans of sweetcorn in a box have a total weight of 4·8 kg. Each can weighs 0·3 kg. How many cans are there in the box?

5. In June a plant grew 1·5 metres. How much did it grow each day in millimetres?

6. A hose delivers 200 ml of water every second. How long will it take to fill a 68·4 litre paddling pool?

7. Twelve pens cost £9. What does one pen cost?

C

1. How many 12 ml tubes of acrylic paint can be filled from 1·5 litres?

2. The total weight of the potatoes in a bag is 5·5 kg. The mean weight is 275 g. How many potatoes are there in the bag?

3. Drinks at a fete cost 65p each. The sale of the drinks raises £83·20. How many drinks are sold?

4. Mince costs £4·00 per kilogram. Otis pays £1·40. How many grams of mince does he buy?

5. A bottle of soy sauce holds 150 ml. How many bottles can be filled from 7·2 litres?

6. With each rotation of his bike's wheel Eric travels 1·8 metres. How many times does the wheel rotate on the 2·25 km journey to school?

I can estimate the size of angles and use a protractor to measure and draw them.

A

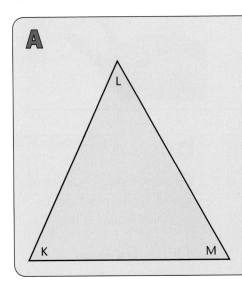

1. Estimate the size of each angle in the triangle to the nearest 10°.

2. Measure the angles.

3. Use a protractor to draw these angles.

   a) 35° **c)** 75° **e)** 15°

   b) 115° **d)** 165° **f)** 145°

4. Draw a triangle with angles of 85° and 40°. Measure the third angle.

B

1. Estimate the size of each angle in the quadrilateral to the nearest 5°C.

2. Measure the angles to the nearest degree.

3. Use a protractor to draw these angles.

   a) 47° **c)** 22° **e)** 83°

   b) 108° **d)** 159° **f)** 136°

4. Draw a quadrilateral with angles of 123°, 76° and 54°. Measure the fourth angle.

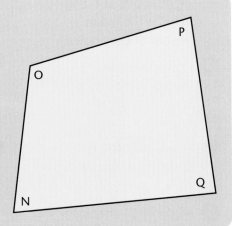

C

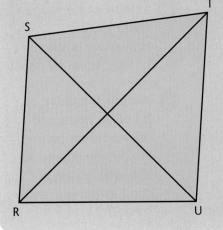

1. Estimate and measure to the nearest degree the angles of these triangles.

   a) RST **c)** RTU

   b) STU **d)** RSU

2. Draw these angles.

   a) 290° **c)** 250° **e)** 237°

   b) 195° **d)** 318° **f)** 336°

3. Draw three different quadrilaterals. Find the sum of the angles of each shape. What do you notice?

I can work out the missing angles in a triangle and around a point.

Examples

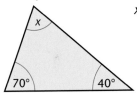

$x + 70° + 40° = 180°$
$x + 110° = 180°$
$x = 70°$

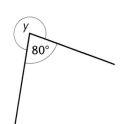

$y + 80° = 360°$
$y = 280°$

A Find the angles marked with the letters.

1. $300°$, a
2. $240°$, b
3. $50°$, c
4. $210°$, d
5. e, $80°$, $50°$
6. $60°$, $90°$, f
7. $70°$, g, $60°$
8. $80°$, h, $40°$

B Find the angles marked with the letters.

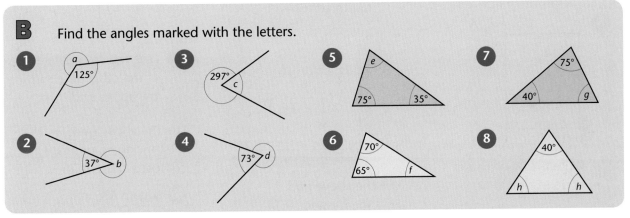

1. a, $125°$
2. $37°$, b
3. $297°$, c
4. $73°$, d
5. e, $75°$, $35°$
6. $70°$, $65°$, f
7. $75°$, $40°$, g
8. $40°$, h, h

C Find the angles marked with the letters.

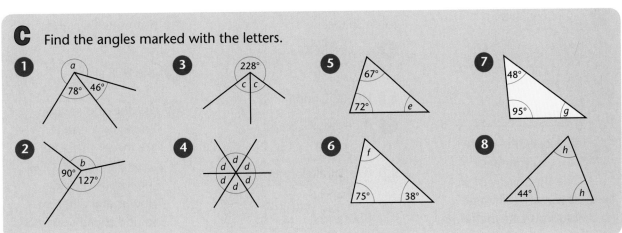

1. a, $78°$, $46°$
2. b, $90°$, $127°$
3. $228°$, c c
4. d d d d d
5. $67°$, $72°$, e
6. f, $75°$, $38°$
7. $48°$, $95°$, g
8. h, $44°$, h

I can read and plot co-ordinates to draw, complete and locate shapes.

The position of a point on a grid is given by its *x* and *y* co-ordinates.

Examples

Point G is (5, 2).

Point E is (2, 5).

Remember:

The *x* co-ordinate always comes first.

A

Use the grid to write:

1 your name

2 your school

3 your favourite subject

4 your favourite TV programme.

5

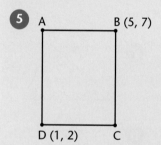

A   B (5, 7)

D (1, 2)   C

Write the co-ordinates of points A and C.

6

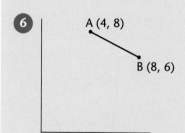

A (4, 8)

B (8, 6)

AB is one side of an isosceles triangle. Give the third vertex. How many different solutions can you find?

B

1 (4, 1), (7, 4) and (4, 7) are three vertices of a square. Give the fourth vertex.

2 (3, 4), (4, 2) and (8, 4) are three vertices of a rectangle. What is the fourth vertex?

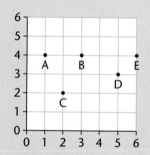

Use the above grid. Find the missing co-ordinates to complete these shapes.

3 square BCD and (☐, ☐)

4 kite BDE and (☐, ☐)

5 rhombus ACB and (☐, ☐)

6 two parallelograms

BDE and (☐, ☐)

BED and (☐, ☐)

C

Examples

Point A is (−3, −1)

Point B is (−2, 3)

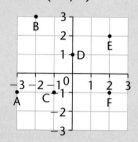

1 Give the co-ordinates of the other letters in the above grid.

Use the above grid. Find the missing co-ordinate to complete these shapes.

2 square ABE and (☐, ☐)

3 rhombus CDE and (☐, ☐)

4 kite BCF and (☐, ☐)

5 Use the above grid. Points C, A and D are three vertices of a parallelogram. Give the fourth vertex. How many different solutions can you find?

I can predict where the image of a shape will be after a reflection.

Examples

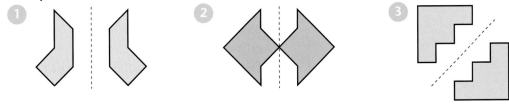

In each of the problems copy the shape and the mirror line and sketch the reflection.

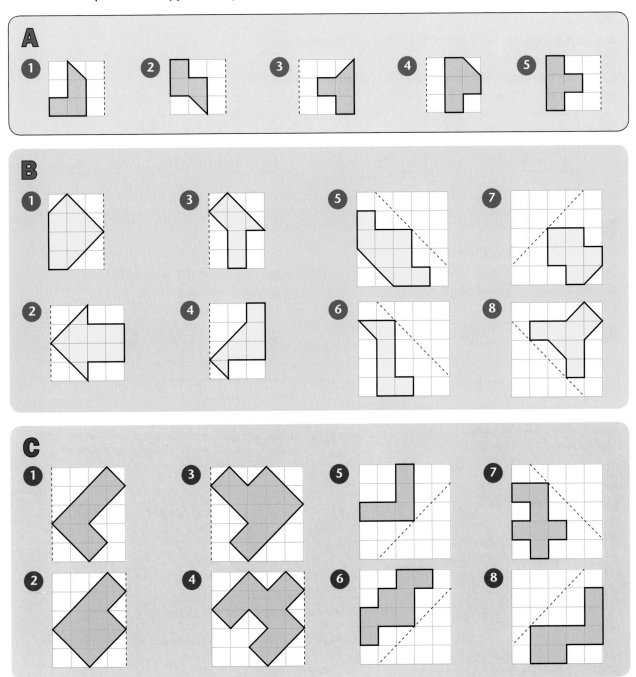

I can predict where the image of a shape will be after a rotation.

Example
A: 90° clockwise
  rotation about (3, 3)
B: 180° rotation
  about (3, 3)

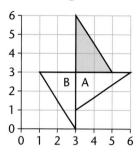

USEFUL TIPS

① 90° rotation – horizontal lines become vertical and vice versa

② 180° rotation – horizontal and vertical lines remain unchanged.

③ Use tracing paper.

A

Use squared paper. For each of the following shapes:
a) copy the shape.
b) rotate the shape 90° about point A in a clockwise direction.
c) rotate the shape 180° about point A.

1
A

2
A

3
A

4
A

B

For each shape predict the co-ordinates of points X and Y after a rotation of:
a) 90° clockwise about point A
b) 180° about point A.

For each shape predict the co-ordinates of points X and Y after a rotation of:
a) 180° about point A
b) 90° about the centre of the shape.

1

2

3

4

Check your predictions by copying each shape on a numbered grid and rotating twice as shown.

C

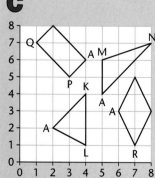

1 Give the positions of K, L, M and N after a rotation of:
   a) 90° clockwise about point A
   b) 180° about point A.

2 Give the positions of P, Q, R and S after a rotation of:
   a) 90° clockwise about point A
   b) 90° about the centre of the shape.

Copy each shape on a separate numbered grid and check your predictions.

I can predict where the image of a shape will be after a translation.

Examples

Translate the red triangle.

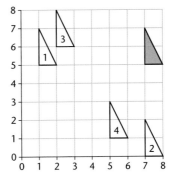

1. left 6 squares (L6)

2. down 5 squares (D5)

3. left 5 squares, up 1 square (L5, U1)

4. left 2 squares, down 4 squares (L2, D4).

A

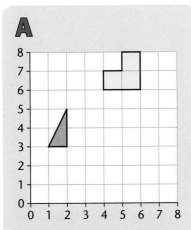

1. Copy the grid and the hexagon. Translate the hexagon three times.

   a) R2

   b) L3

   c) D3

   Give the co-ordinates of the new position for each shape.

2. Draw a new grid and the triangle. Translate the triangle three times.

   a) U2

   b) R4

   c) L1

   Give the co-ordinates of the new position for each shape.

B

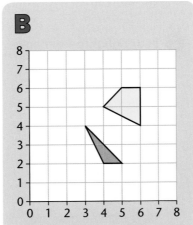

1. Give the co-ordinates of the new position of the above triangle after a translation of:

   a) L2 D2   c) L3 U4

   b) R1 U2   d) R3 D1.

   Copy the grid and draw the translations to check.

2. Predict the co-ordinates of the new position of the above quadrilateral after a translation of:

   a) R1 U2   c) R2 D4

   b) L3 D3   d) L4 U1.

   Draw a new grid and translate the quadrilateral to check.

C

1. Draw a new grid. Plot these points. (3, 3) (2, 5) (4, 6) Join them up to make a triangle.

2. Predict the co-ordinates of the triangle after a translation of:

   a) L2 U1   c) L1 D3

   b) R4 D3   d) R3 U2.

   Draw the translations to check.

3. Draw a new grid. Plot these points and join them up in the order given. (3, 4) (4, 5) (6, 3) (5, 2) (3, 4)

4. Predict the co-ordinates of the rectangle after a translation of:

   a) R2 D2   c) R1 U3

   b) L3 U2   d) L2 D1.

   Draw the translations to check.

I can translate information and look for patterns to solve problems.

A

1. The teams in a football league play each other once only. When there were three teams in the League there were 3 games.

   Rovers v Wolves
   Wolves v Lions
   Lions v Rovers

   When there were four teams there were 6 games.

   Rovers v Wolves
   Jaguars v Lions
   Rovers v Jaguars
   Lions v Wolves
   Wolves v Jaguars
   Lions v Rovers

   How many games will there be when the League has:

   a) 5 teams
   b) 6 teams
   c) 7 teams?

2. Ed has 50 straws. He makes equilateral triangles and squares. He has no straws left over. How many triangles has he made and how many squares?
   There are four possible answers.
   Can you find them?

B

1. Look at Question 1 in Section A.
   How many games will there be when the League has:

   a) 10 teams
   b) 20 teams?

2. Return flights are made between airports. Between three airports there are 6 flights.

   How many flights are there between:

   a) 4 airports
   b) 5 airports
   c) 10 airports?

3. Write a formula for the number of flights (*f*) made between (*a*) airports.

4. Jo has 100 straws. She makes heptagons and octagons. She has 2 straws left over. How many has she made of each shape?

5. Find two ways of using 100 straws to make heptagons and octagons so that there are no straws left over.

C

1. Return bus journeys are made between villages each morning and afternoon. Four journeys are made between 2 villages.

   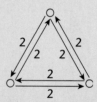

   Twelve journeys are made between 3 villages.

   How many journeys are made between:

   a) 4 villages
   b) 5 villages
   c) 6 villages
   d) 10 villages?

2. Write a formula for the number of journeys (*j*) made between *v* villages.

3. Lollies cost 90p. Ice creams cost £1·30. Lily buys lollies and ice creams for exactly £25. How many lollies does she buy and how many ice creams?
   Find both possible solutions.

I can write a larger whole number as a fraction of a smaller number and simplify fractions by cancelling.

Examples

How many times larger is 20 than 6?

$20 \div 6 = 3\frac{2}{6}$

$\qquad = 3\frac{1}{3}$

20 is $3\frac{1}{3}$ times larger than 6.

Write $\frac{12}{20}$ in its simplest form.

Highest common factor of 12 and 20 is 4.

$\dfrac{12}{20} \dfrac{\div 4}{\div 4} = \dfrac{3}{5} \qquad \dfrac{12}{20} = \dfrac{3}{5}$

A

1 ○○ ○○ ○○ ○○ ○
○○

How many times larger is 9 than 2?

2 ○○○○○ ○○○○○ ○○
○○○○○

How many times larger is 12 than 5?

3 ○○○ ○○○ ○○○ ○
○○○

How many times larger is 10 than 3?

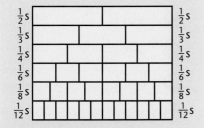

Use the fraction chart.
Copy and complete.

4 $\dfrac{10}{12} = \dfrac{\square}{6}$ **8** $\dfrac{1}{4} = \dfrac{\square}{12}$

5 $\dfrac{8}{12} = \dfrac{\square}{3}$ **9** $\dfrac{6}{8} = \dfrac{\square}{12}$

6 $\dfrac{6}{8} = \dfrac{\square}{4}$ **10** $\dfrac{1}{2} = \dfrac{\square}{8}$

7 $\dfrac{2}{6} = \dfrac{\square}{3}$ **11** $\dfrac{2}{3} = \dfrac{\square}{6}$

B

How many times larger is:

1 26 than 6

2 40 than 15

3 75 than 20

4 34 than 12

5 £100 than £40

6 1 kg than 120 g

7 2 litres than 600 ml

8 5 m than 40 cm?

How many hours are there in:

9 150 minutes

10 105 minutes

11 290 minutes

12 220 minutes?

Cancel each fraction into its simplest form.

13 $\frac{4}{12}$ **21** $\frac{3}{9}$

14 $\frac{2}{8}$ **22** $\frac{8}{10}$

15 $\frac{6}{9}$ **23** $\frac{15}{18}$

16 $\frac{4}{10}$ **24** $\frac{12}{16}$

17 $\frac{12}{20}$ **25** $\frac{25}{100}$

18 $\frac{6}{15}$ **26** $\frac{9}{12}$

19 $\frac{30}{100}$ **27** $\frac{18}{30}$

20 $\frac{6}{12}$ **28** $\frac{16}{24}$

C

How many times larger is:

1 0·5 litres than 80 ml

2 £2.00 than 35p

3 1 kg than 225 g

4 1 m than 16 cm?

Find

5 $\frac{7}{4}$ of 200 g

6 $\frac{12}{5}$ of 75 cm

7 $\frac{11}{3}$ of 45p

8 $\frac{13}{8}$ of £6·00

One mile is 1·6 km.
How many miles are there in:

9 2 km   **11** 4 km

10 3 km   **12** 5 km?

Cancel each fraction into its lowest form.

13 $\frac{10}{14}$ **21** $\frac{12}{36}$

14 $\frac{45}{50}$ **22** $\frac{85}{100}$

15 $\frac{30}{48}$ **23** $\frac{24}{80}$

16 $\frac{36}{100}$ **24** $\frac{54}{72}$

17 $\frac{14}{20}$ **25** $\frac{20}{35}$

18 $\frac{18}{24}$ **26** $\frac{32}{40}$

19 $\frac{350}{1000}$ **27** $\frac{18}{21}$

20 $\frac{48}{60}$ **28** $\frac{625}{1000}$

I can order fractions by converting them to fractions with a common denominator or by using a calculator to find the decimal equivalents.

Examples

Arrange $\frac{1}{2}$, $\frac{3}{5}$, $\frac{8}{20}$ in ascending order.

Find a common denominator → 10

$\frac{1}{2} = \frac{5}{10}$ $\frac{3}{5} = \frac{6}{10}$ $\frac{8}{20} = \frac{4}{10}$

The correct order is $\frac{8}{20}$, $\frac{1}{2}$, $\frac{3}{5}$.

Arrange $\frac{2}{3}$, $\frac{7}{11}$, $\frac{5}{8}$ in ascending order.

Use a calculator and round to the nearest $\frac{1}{100}$.

$2 \div 3 = 0.67$ $7 \div 11 = 0.64$ $5 \div 8 = 0.63$

The correct order is $\frac{5}{8}$, $\frac{7}{11}$, $\frac{2}{3}$.

A

1 Which of the fractions in the box are:

   a) equal to one half

   b) less than one half

   c) greater than one half?

$\frac{1}{6}$	$\frac{6}{10}$	$\frac{3}{8}$	$\frac{50}{100}$	$\frac{4}{9}$
$\frac{3}{5}$	$\frac{8}{16}$	$\frac{11}{20}$	$\frac{5}{12}$	$\frac{20}{50}$

Write > or < in each box.

2 $\frac{3}{8} \square \frac{1}{4}$ **6** $\frac{3}{4} \square \frac{10}{12}$

3 $\frac{1}{2} \square \frac{3}{5}$ **7** $\frac{5}{6} \square \frac{2}{3}$

4 $\frac{3}{6} \square \frac{2}{3}$ **8** $\frac{4}{15} \square \frac{2}{5}$

5 $\frac{2}{5} \square \frac{3}{10}$ **9** $\frac{3}{4} \square \frac{11}{16}$

10 Use a calculator. Arrange these fractions in order, smallest first.

   $\frac{5}{8}$ $\frac{13}{20}$ $\frac{9}{15}$ $\frac{16}{25}$

11 Write a fraction larger than $\frac{9}{10}$.

12 Write a fraction smaller than $\frac{1}{10}$.

B

Arrange in ascending order.

1 $\frac{1}{3}$, $\frac{1}{4}$, $\frac{2}{12}$

2 $\frac{1}{2}$, $\frac{4}{10}$, $\frac{11}{20}$

3 $\frac{2}{3}$, $\frac{4}{5}$, $\frac{11}{15}$

4 $\frac{9}{12}$, $\frac{4}{6}$, $\frac{1}{2}$

5 $\frac{1}{5}$, $\frac{3}{10}$, $\frac{1}{2}$

6 $\frac{1}{4}$, $\frac{2}{5}$, $\frac{3}{20}$

Find a number which lies between:

7 $\frac{1}{7}$ and $\frac{2}{7}$

8 $\frac{2}{3}$ and $\frac{1}{2}$

9 $\frac{3}{4}$ and $\frac{5}{8}$

10 $\frac{3}{10}$ and $\frac{2}{5}$

11 $\frac{3}{4}$ and $\frac{5}{6}$

12 1 and $\frac{4}{5}$.

Use a calculator to arrange in ascending order.

13 $\frac{2}{3}$, $\frac{4}{7}$, $\frac{5}{9}$

14 $\frac{9}{11}$, $\frac{13}{15}$, $\frac{5}{6}$

15 $\frac{7}{18}$, $\frac{5}{12}$, $\frac{3}{8}$

16 $\frac{6}{13}$, $\frac{3}{7}$, $\frac{9}{24}$

C

Arrange in ascending order.

1 $\frac{1}{2}$, $\frac{4}{12}$, $\frac{3}{4}$, $\frac{2}{3}$

2 $\frac{3}{8}$, $\frac{2}{5}$, $\frac{1}{4}$, $\frac{3}{10}$

3 $\frac{6}{10}$, $\frac{3}{4}$, $\frac{1}{2}$, $\frac{2}{5}$

4 $\frac{1}{3}$, $\frac{1}{4}$, $\frac{2}{9}$, $\frac{1}{6}$

5 $\frac{5}{6}$, $\frac{1}{2}$, $\frac{2}{3}$, $\frac{4}{9}$

6 $\frac{2}{3}$, $\frac{5}{8}$, $\frac{3}{4}$, $\frac{3}{6}$

Find the number which lies halfway between:

7 $\frac{1}{2}$ and $\frac{2}{5}$

8 $\frac{4}{9}$ and $\frac{2}{3}$

9 $\frac{1}{4}$ and $\frac{1}{2}$

10 $\frac{2}{3}$ and $\frac{5}{6}$

11 $\frac{5}{12}$ and $\frac{1}{4}$

12 $\frac{1}{4}$ and $\frac{1}{3}$.

Use a calculator to arrange in ascending order.

13 $\frac{5}{7}$, $\frac{8}{11}$, $\frac{5}{6}$, $\frac{7}{9}$

14 $\frac{2}{3}$, $\frac{9}{14}$, $\frac{5}{8}$, $\frac{5}{9}$

15 $\frac{4}{13}$, $\frac{2}{7}$, $\frac{5}{16}$, $\frac{3}{8}$

16 $\frac{2}{9}$, $\frac{4}{11}$, $\frac{1}{4}$, $\frac{7}{25}$

I can solve problems involving ratio and proportion.

Examples

There are 2 boys for every 5 girls at a swimming club. There are 49 children at the club. How many are girls?

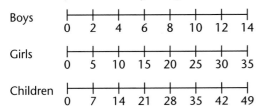

Boys
0 2 4 6 8 10 12 14

Girls
0 5 10 15 20 25 30 35

Children
0 7 14 21 28 35 42 49

Answer   *35 girls*

A recipe uses 500 g of meat for 4 people. How much meat is needed for:

a) 3 people   b) 10 people?

Answers

a) $(500\,g ÷ 4) × 3 = 125\,g × 3$
$= 375\,g$

b) $(500\,g × 2) + (500\,g ÷ 2) = 1000\,g + 250\,g$
$= 1·25\,kg$

A

EGG FRIED RICE
250 g rice
2 eggs
6 spring onions
4 large mushrooms
Serves 4

1 Rewrite the above ingredients for:

a) 2 people

b) 8 people.

A necklace is made using this pattern of beads.

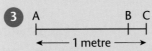

2 How many red beads are there for every:

a) 20 yellow beads

b) 36 yellow beads?

3 How many yellow beads are there if there are:

a) 12 red beads

b) 42 beads altogether?

4 A farmer has 5 sheep for every 2 cows. He has 30 sheep. How many cows does he have?

B

MACARONI CHEESE
160 g cheese
200 g macaroni
60 g flour
40 g butter
500 ml milk
Serves 4

1 Rewrite the above ingredients for:

a) 3 people

b) 10 people.

2 A car uses 150 ml of petrol every minute. How long will it take for it to use 4·5 litres?

3

A   B C

← 1 metre →

AB is four times the length of BC. How long is AB?

4 There are 80 red and green apples in a box. Two in every five are green. How many are red?

5 Altogether Jude and Matt have 60 marbles. Jude has twice as many as Matt. How many does Matt have?

C

CHEESE MUFFINS
250 g flour
20 g caster sugar
60 g cheese
200 ml milk
Makes 10

1 Rewrite the above ingredients for

a) 15 muffins

b) 8 muffins.

2 A ribbon is 1·6 m long. It is cut into two lengths. The longer ribbon is one and a half times the length of the shorter one. How long is each ribbon?

3 Five in every eight of the 120 cars passing the school had no passengers. How many cars had no passengers?

4 On January 1st there were three 10 year olds to every two 11 year olds in Year 6. There are 90 children in Year 6. How many were 11 before January 1st?

I can find equivalent fractions, decimals and percentages.

Per cent means out of 100.
Percentages are fractions with a denominator of 100.
The symbol for per cent is %.

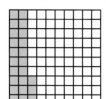

$\frac{23}{100} = 23\%$

To express fractions as percentages, change them to equivalent fractions with denominators of 100.

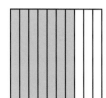

$\frac{7}{10} = \frac{70}{100} = 70\%$

$\frac{1}{2} = \frac{50}{100} = 50\%$

To express decimals as percentages, multiply by 100.

$0{\cdot}2 = (0{\cdot}2 \times 100)\%$
$= 20\%$

$0{\cdot}53 = (0{\cdot}53 \times 100)\%$
$= 53\%$

It is useful to know that:

$\frac{1}{100} = 0{\cdot}01 = 1\%, \quad \frac{2}{100} = 0{\cdot}02 = 2\%,$ etc

$\frac{1}{10} = 0{\cdot}1 = 10\%, \quad \frac{2}{10} = 0{\cdot}2 = 20\%,$ etc

$\frac{1}{4} = 25\%, \quad \frac{1}{2} = 50\%, \quad \frac{3}{4} = 75\%$

A

Express each shaded area as:

a) a fraction

b) a decimal

c) a percentage.

1   **6**

2   **7**

3 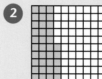   **8**

4    **9**

5 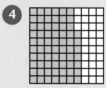   **10**

11 What percentage of the boxes contain:

   a) ticks   **b)** crosses   **c)** circles?

12 What percentage of the 20 boxes are blank?

B

1. Copy and complete the table.

Fractions	Decimals	%ages
$\frac{3}{10}$	0·3	30%
		46%
		25%
		70%
	0·09	
	0·6	
	0·5	
	0·83	
$\frac{3}{100}$		
$\frac{11}{50}$		
$\frac{7}{20}$		
$\frac{3}{25}$		

What percentage could be used in each of these sentences.

2. Fay scored 38 out of 50 in her History Test.

3. Two fifths of the children have fair hair.

4. Seven in every ten voters supported the winning candidate.

5. Half the chocolates have hard centres.

6. The football team won 12 out of the 25 matches played.

7. Two in every hundred mothers gave birth to twins.

8. Michael Owen was on target with 4 out of his 5 shots at goal.

9. Three quarters of the choir were boys.

10. It rained on eleven days in every twenty.

C

Write each fraction as:
a) a decimal
b) a percentage.

1. $\frac{9}{10}$
2. $\frac{23}{50}$
3. $\frac{3}{5}$
4. $\frac{78}{100}$
5. $\frac{7}{25}$
6. $\frac{198}{200}$
7. $\frac{9}{20}$
8. $\frac{470}{1000}$

Write each percentage as:
a) a fraction in its simplest form
b) a decimal.

9. 62%
10. 30%
11. 15%
12. 43%
13. 64%
14. 80%
15. 12·5%
16. 2·5%

17. Copy and complete the table showing the results of a football team's penalty competition.

Name	Shots	Goals	%age scored	%age missed
Joy	25	16		
Di	24	15		
Pat	20	13		
Sue	30		70%	
Fay	36		75%	
Eve	26			50%
Liz	25			40%

18. Use squared paper. Draw an 8 × 5 grid of 40 boxes.
   a) Put ticks in 25% of the boxes.
   b) Put crosses in 40% of the boxes.
   c) Put circles in 15% of the boxes.

Examples

$\frac{1}{8}$ of 640	$\frac{5}{8}$ of 640	10% of 40	30% of 40	5% of 40
640 ÷ 8	($\frac{1}{8}$ of 640) × 5	$\frac{1}{10}$ of 40	(10% of 40) × 3	(10% of 40) ÷ 2
80	80 × 5	40 ÷ 10	4 × 3	4 ÷ 2
	400	4	12	2

A

Find

1. $\frac{1}{4}$ of 24
2. $\frac{1}{6}$ of 48
3. $\frac{1}{3}$ of 21 cm
4. $\frac{1}{5}$ of 25p
5. $\frac{1}{7}$ of 42 m

6. $\frac{3}{5}$ of 40
7. $\frac{7}{8}$ of 16
8. $\frac{2}{3}$ of 15p
9. $\frac{4}{9}$ of £27
10. $\frac{3}{4}$ of 36 m

11. 10% of 50
12. 10% of 120
13. 10% of 60p
14. 10% of 1 m
15. 10% of £2

16. 20% of 70
17. 50% of 32
18. 30% of 500 g
19. 25% of 12 m
20. 20% of 400 ml

B

Work out

1. $\frac{5}{6}$ of 42
2. $\frac{4}{9}$ of 36
3. $\frac{6}{7}$ of 49
4. $\frac{2}{3}$ of £1·20
5. $\frac{3}{5}$ of 60 cm
6. $\frac{5}{8}$ of £72

7. 50% of 27
8. 20% of 140
9. 1% of 350
10. 30% of 250 g
11. 5% of 800 ml
12. 40% of £6·00

13. A test was marked out of 60. Eden got two thirds right. Oscar got 60%. Who had done better and by how many marks?

14. A school bought 300 pens. Three fifths were given out. 5% were faulty and returned. How many pens were left?

15. Forty per cent of the 120 children had school dinners. How many children did not have school dinners?

16. Forty-two children in Year 6 were going to their nearest Secondary School. This was 75% of the year group. How many children were in Year 6?

17. A farmer has 160 eggs. Three eighths are large and 30% are medium. How many are small?

C

Work out

1. $\frac{5}{6}$ of 300
2. $\frac{7}{9}$ of 4·5 m
3. $\frac{16}{25}$ of 1 litre
4. $\frac{4}{7}$ of £1·40
5. $\frac{5}{12}$ of 3·6 kg
6. $\frac{3}{8}$ of 1 km

7. 90% of £6·80
8. 3% of £150
9. 11% of 2 litres
10. 99% of £5
11. 15% of 0·5 kg
12. 8% of 2·5 m

13. There are 180 people watching a film. 65% are children. Two ninths are women. How many men are in the audience?

14. Hassan buys a brand new car. One year later it is valued at £6300. This is 30% less than the price of the new car. What was that price?

15. Esther leaves £5000 in a savings account which earns 3·5% interest each year. How much interest is earned in the first year?

16. Exactly 2400 people vote in an election. The winning candidate polls 40%. The second candidate gets three eighths of the votes. How many votes were shared by the other candidates?

I can use and order decimal numbers with up to three places.

Examples

Arrange 1·4, 1·41, 1·141 and 1 in ascending order.

Write in column	Put in zeros	Arrange in order
1·4	1·400	1
1·41	1·410	1·141
1·141	1·141	1·4
1	1·000	1·41

What number is halfway between 2·5 and 2·75?

$2·75 - 2·5 = 0·25$

$0·25 ÷ 2 = 0·125$

$2·5 + 0·125 = 2·625$

Answer   2·625

A

Copy and complete by writing > or < in the box.

1. 2·55 ☐ 5·2

2. 6·7 ☐ 6·34

3. 4·18 ☐ 4·8

4. 7·59 ☐ 5·79

What number lies halfway between:

5. 7 and 8

6. 3·56 and 3·6

7. 2·42 and 2·48

8. 6 and 6·5?

Copy and complete.

9. $0·35 + 0·4 = ☐$

10. $1·24 + 0·03 = ☐$

11. $3·16 + ☐ = 3·66$

12. $0·92 + ☐ = 0·99$

13. $5·76 - 0·02 = ☐$

14. $2·91 - 0·6 = ☐$

15. $0·33 - ☐ = 0·03$

16. $4·07 - ☐ = 4·0$

B

Arrange these decimals in ascending order.

1. 8·247, 8·47, 0·847, 84·7

2. 6·119, 1·169, 6·19, 1·69

3. 3·2, 0·37, 0·307, 2·07

4. 4·66, 4·565, 5·644, 5·446

What number lies halfway between:

5. 4·382 and 4·388

6. 1·31 and 1·32

7. 0·145 and 0·155

8. 1·9 and 1·95?

Copy and complete.

9. $0·932 + 0·004 = ☐$

10. $2·387 + 0·3 = ☐$

11. $5·201 + ☐ = 5·208$

12. $1·054 + ☐ = 1·06$

13. $0·923 - 0·5 = ☐$

14. $4·645 - 0·002 = ☐$

15. $1·086 - ☐ = 1·006$

16. $0·714 - ☐ = 0·71$

C

Arrange these decimals in ascending order.

1. 2·222, 2·2, 22·2, 2·22

2. 1·414, 1·44, 1·114, 1·4

3. 6·606, 6·66, 6·6, 6·06

4. 1·717, 1·7, 1·17, 1·117

What number lies halfway between:

5. 0·916 and 0·93

6. 2 and 2·25

7. 4·63 and 4·7

8. 0·25 and 0·2?

Copy and complete.

9. $0·258 + ☐ = 0·264$

10. $5·436 + ☐ = 6·136$

11. $1·927 + ☐ = 1·942$

12. $0·851 + ☐ = 1·031$

13. $4·352 - ☐ = 4·272$

14. $8·197 - ☐ = 6·897$

15. $2·046 - ☐ = 1·996$

16. $10·1 - ☐ = 9·998$

I can use place value and partitioning to calculate mentally.

A

Copy and complete.

1. $2.7 + 1.3 = \boxed{}$
2. $0.5 + 0.6 = \boxed{}$
3. $5 - 1.4 = \boxed{}$
4. $0.4 - 0.03 = \boxed{}$

5. $0.2 \times 8 = \boxed{}$
6. $1.3 \times 2 = \boxed{}$
7. $15 \div 100 = \boxed{}$
8. $3.0 \div 6 = \boxed{}$

9. $0.08 + \boxed{} = 0.12$
10. $3.5 + \boxed{} = 6$
11. $9 - \boxed{} = 8.7$
12. $4.3 - \boxed{} = 2.8$

13. $0.07 \times \boxed{} = 0.42$
14. $0.36 \times \boxed{} = 3.6$
15. $2.4 \div \boxed{} = 0.6$
16. $0.21 \div \boxed{} = 0.07$

17. $\boxed{} + 0.7 = 1.6$
18. $\boxed{} + 0.21 = 0.5$
19. $\boxed{} - 0.9 = 4.3$
20. $\boxed{} - 0.07 = 1.83$

21. $\boxed{} \times 4 = 0.36$
22. $\boxed{} \times 100 = 8$
23. $\boxed{} \div 10 = 0.7$
24. $\boxed{} \div 5 = 0.8$

B

Copy and complete.

1. $9.57 + 2.43 = \boxed{}$
2. $0.7 + 0.735 = \boxed{}$
3. $8 - 5.72 = \boxed{}$
4. $4.6 - 1.37 = \boxed{}$

5. $0.17 \times 4 = \boxed{}$
6. $0.038 \times 5 = \boxed{}$
7. $87 \div 1000 = \boxed{}$
8. $0.03 \div 5 = \boxed{}$

9. $0.006 + \boxed{} = 0.03$
10. $1.36 + \boxed{} = 3$
11. $3.59 - \boxed{} = 1.79$
12. $6.3 - \boxed{} = 6.288$

13. $0.009 \times \boxed{} = 9$
14. $0.096 \times \boxed{} = 0.198$
15. $0.48 \div \boxed{} = 0.16$
16. $2.1 \div \boxed{} = 0.35$

17. $\boxed{} + 3.5 = 4.76$
18. $\boxed{} + 0.013 = 0.07$
19. $\boxed{} - 3.01 = 5.09$
20. $\boxed{} - 0.029 = 0.041$

21. $\boxed{} \times 4 = 0.76$
22. $\boxed{} \times 9 = 0.135$
23. $\boxed{} \div 100 = 0.052$
24. $\boxed{} \div 5 = 1.9$

C

Copy and complete.

1. $0.63 + 0.664 = \boxed{}$
2. $0.906 + 0.104 = \boxed{}$
3. $1.1 - 0.247 = \boxed{}$
4. $7.421 - 2.38 = \boxed{}$

5. $0.08 \times 50 = \boxed{}$
6. $0.304 \times 7 = \boxed{}$
7. $0.438 \div 6 = \boxed{}$
8. $3.6 \div 60 = \boxed{}$

9. $3.575 + \boxed{} = 5$
10. $0.729 + \boxed{} = 2.469$
11. $2.158 - \boxed{} = 0.968$
12. $10 - \boxed{} = 5.439$

13. $0.125 \times \boxed{} = 0.75$
14. $0.204 \times \boxed{} = 20.4$
15. $3.43 \div \boxed{} = 0.49$
16. $0.12 \div \boxed{} = 0.004$

17. $\boxed{} + 0.005 = 0.05$
18. $\boxed{} + 2.43 = 6.8$
19. $\boxed{} - 0.244 = 0.006$
20. $\boxed{} - 0.053 = 4.157$

21. $\boxed{} \times 8 = 0.216$
22. $\boxed{} \times 20 = 7.2$
23. $\boxed{} \div 4 = 0.315$
24. $\boxed{} \div 8 = 0.125$

I can use linked facts to solve word problems mentally.

Example
Eight cans of dog food
cost £3·20.
What does one can cost?

$32 \div 8 = 4$
$£3·20 \div 8 = £0·40$

One can costs 40p.

A

$$73 - 28 = 45$$

Use the above fact to work out the following facts.

1. $7·3 - 4·5$
2. $4·5 + 2·8$
3. $0·73 - 0·28$
4. $0·28 + 0·45$

5. $7·3 - 2·8$
6. $0·73 - 0·45$
7. $0·45 + 0·28$
8. $2·8 + 4·5$

$$48 \div 6 = 8$$

Use the above fact to work out the following facts.

9. $4·8 \div 8$
10. $0·48 \div 8$
11. $0·8 \times 6$
12. $0·06 \times 8$

13. $4·8 \div 6$
14. $0·48 \div 6$
15. $0·08 \times 6$
16. $0·6 \times 8$

B

Use each given fact to find linked facts involving decimals.

1. $56 + 38 = 94$
2. $9 \times 4 = 36$
3. $80 - 63 = 17$
4. $5 \times 6 = 30$

5. One ice cream costs £0·90. What do three ice creams cost?

6. Salma buys a CD for £3·90 and a game for £4·80. How much has she spent?

7. A box holds 5·5 kg of apples. 2·9 kg is eaten. How much is left?

8. A jug holds 1·2 litres of orange juice. All of the juice is poured equally into six glasses. How much orange is there in each glass?

9. Sharon walks 8·4 km every day for a week. How far does she walk altogether?

C

Use each given fact to find linked facts involving decimals.

1. $175 \div 7 = 25$
2. $143 - 89 = 54$

3. One parcel weighs 1·38 kg. A second weighs 0·47 kg. What is their combined weight?

4. A plank is 3·2 metres long. It is cut into five equal lengths. How long is each length?

5. Cliff has £6·40. He spends £3·95. How much does he have left?

6. A carton of juice holds 0·075 litres. How much does a pack of 8 cartons hold?

7. A sailing race is four circuits of a 3·8 mile course. How long is the race?

I can use a calculator to find examples to match a general statement.

A

Use a calculator to find four examples that match each statement.

1 Multiplying a number by 0·5 is the same as halving it.

2 Dividing a number by 10 moves every digit one place to the right.

3 Dividing a number by 0·1 is the same as multiplying by 10.

4 The product of two decimal fractions is smaller than either of the two numbers.

5 Finding 10% of a number is the same as dividing by 10.

6 To multiply by 100, move every digit two places to the left.

B

Use a calculator to find four examples that match each statement.

1 Dividing a number by 0·25 is the same as multiplying it by 4.

2 Multiplying a number by 0·01 makes it 100 times as small.

3 Finding 10% of a number is the same as multiplying by 0·1.

4 The square of a decimal fraction is smaller than that number.

5 To multiply a decimal number by 50, move every digit two places to the left and halve the answer.

6 To find 1% of a number, move every digit two places to the right.

C

Use a calculator to find four examples that match each statement.

1 Multiplying a number by 0·001 makes it 1000 times as big.

2 Dividing a number by 0·05 is the same as multiplying by 20.

3 Finding 30% of a number is the same as moving every digit one place to the right and multiplying by 3.

4 The product of a decimal fraction and a whole number is smaller than the whole number.

5 To multiply a number by 1·5, increase it by one half of the number.

6 Finding 2% of a number is the same as multiplying by 0·01 and doubling the answer.

I can use efficient written methods to solve word problems.

Example

A cycle race is 117 km long.
It consists of five laps of a circular route.
How long is one lap?

One lap is 23·4 km long.

```
    117
  −100   (5 × 20)
  ─────
     17
  −  15   (5 × 3)
  ─────
      2
  −   2   (5 × 0·4)
  ─────
      0
```
Answer 23·4

A

1 Great Britain has an area of 229·8 thousand km². Ireland has an area of 84·4 thousand km². How much larger is Great Britain?

2 A regular pentagon has a perimeter of 34 cm. How long is one side?

3 One can of paint holds 3·8 litres. How much will six cans hold?

4 Mrs. Lee weighs 55·3 kg. Mr. Lee weighs 19·8 kg more. What does Mr. Lee weigh?

5 One mile is 1·6 kilometres. What is eight miles in kilometres?

6 Four train tickets cost £94. What does one ticket cost?

B

1 Eight identical parcels have a total weight of 11·6 kg. What does one parcel weigh?

2 A carpet costs £15 per square metre. What will it cost to carpet a room 4 metres long and 3·4 metres wide?

3 A prize of £213 is shared between five people. How much will they receive each?

4 One gallon is 4·55 litres. What is six gallons in litres?

5 Earth orbits the Sun at a distance of 148·6 million km. Mars' orbit is 227·3 million km from the Sun. How much nearer to the Sun is the Earth than Mars?

6 A baker mixes 2·85 kg of white flour with 1·75 kg of brown flour. How much flour is there altogether?

C

1 Twelve bags of hamster food weigh 16·2 kg. What does one bag weigh?

2 A room is 3·6 m long and 2·4 m wide. How much will it cost to carpet the room at £14 per square metre?

3 A builder has 186 kg of cement. He uses one eighth. How much does he have left?

It is estimated that in 2021 the male population of the UK will be 31·943 million and the female population 32·784 million.

4 How much bigger is the estimated female population than the male?

5 What is the estimated UK population in 2021?

6 A watering can holds 3·34 litres. It is one quarter full. How much water is in the can?

I can solve multi-step problems.

Example

A lorry is 2·48 metres wide.
The gap between the lorry and
the side of the road is 28·5 cm on
either side. How wide is the road?

28·5 cm × 2 = 57 cm
2·48 m = 248 cm
248 cm + 57 cm = 305 cm
The road is 3·05 m wide.

A

1. The perimeter of a square field is 360 m. What is its area?

2. A bottle of medicine contains 0·15 litres. Paige takes 20 ml every day. How many bottles will she need in June?

3. Cherie buys two pens for £1·45 each and three pencils for 25p each. How much does she spend?

4. There is 2 litres of milk in a bottle. 750 ml is poured into a jug. How many 200 ml glasses can be filled from the milk left in the bottle?

5. Six equal lengths are cut from 2 m of string. 20 cm is left over. How long are the lengths of string?

6. Large boxes weigh 2·5 kg. Small boxes weigh 800 g. What is the total weight in kilograms of six large and six small boxes?

B

1. How many seconds are there in 12 hours?

2. George swims 4 km every day. The pool is 50 m in length. How many lengths does he swim in one week?

3. Eight 350 ml beakers are filled from a full 4·5 litre flask of tea. How much tea is left in the flask?

4. A ribbon is 10 metres long. 4·2 m is cut off. How many 60 cm lengths can be cut from the remaining ribbon?

5. A box of six eggs weighs 0·46 kg. The box weighs 40 g. What is the mean weight of the eggs?

6. Between them Jack and Joyce have £63·40. Jack has £12·78 more than Joyce. How much do they each have?

C

1. A garage entrance is 2·1 m wide. The car is 1·64 m wide. How many centimetres are there between each wall and the car?

2. A pilot's training flight lasts 1 hour 25 minutes. How many flights will he make before he has completed 50 hours flying time?

3. A punch bowl contains 1·7 litres of drink. 700 ml is added. The drink is shared among eight people. How much do they each have in millilitres?

4. Nuts cost £3·80 per kg. Marco buys 650 g. How much change will he receive from £5?

5. Scott opens his parachute 750 m above ground level. He has already fallen seven ninths of the way to the ground. How high was the plane flying when he jumped?

I can solve word problems and suggest word problems to match a given calculation.

Example
Three men sit on a bench. They have a combined weight of 262·2 kg. Bill and Harry both weigh 84·8 kg. What does Joe weigh?

$84·8 \times 2 = 169·6$
$262·2 - 169·6 = 92·6$

Joe weighs 92·6 kg.

A

1. Twenty pills weigh 10 g altogether. What does one pill weigh?

2. A roll of tape is 6 metres long. Lengths of 1·3 m and 0·8 m are cut off. How much tape is left?

3. There are five potatoes in a bag. Their mean weight is 0·4 kg. What do the potatoes weigh altogether?

4. A tea urn holds 5 litres. Six 0·2 litre cups and four 0·3 litre mugs are filled from the urn. How much tea is left?

Write a word problem for each calculation.

5. $7·8 + 0·6 = 8·4$

6. $3·6 \times 8 = 28·8$

7. $5·9 - 2·5 = 3·4$

8. $11·5 \div 2 = 5·75$

B

1. A rectangular room has a perimeter of 18·4 m and a longest side of 5·2 m. What is the area of the room?

2. A box of 50 matches weighs 32 g. The empty box weighs 8 g. What is the weight of one match?

3. A snake slithers 12 m in four minutes. What is its average speed in metres per second?

4. Jo buys forty 0·75 kg cans of cat food. Every day Jack eats 0·65 kg and Bailey eats 0·55 kg. How long will the cans last?

5. A petrol pump delivers 17·2 litres in 40 seconds. How much petrol is delivered every second?

Write a word problem for each calculation.

6. $5·7 - 0·68 = 5·02$

7. $4·31 + 2·4 = 6·71$

8. $6·4 \div 0·2 = 32$

9. $0·46 \times 5 = 2·3$

C

1. The total weight of twenty ants is 3 g. What is their mean weight?

2. A saucepan contains 1·6 litres of boiling water. 0·137 litres evaporates before 0·25 litres is added. How much water is now in the saucepan?

3. The 200 pins in a packet weigh 25 g. What does one pin weigh?

4. Zena's heart beats once every 0·75 seconds. What is her heart rate in beats per minute?

5. A square field has an area of 0·25 km². What is the perimeter of the field?

Write a word problem for each calculation.

6. $1·625 \times 6 = 9·75$

7. $3·59 - 0·225 = 3·365$

8. $9·648 + 0·62 = 10·268$

9. $1·7 \div 2·5 = 0·68$

I can tabulate results systematically to find all possible solutions to a problem.

A

1

T   U

67 can be made on an abacus using exactly 13 beads. Five other 2-digit numbers can be made on an abacus using 13 beads. Can you find them?

2 How many different 2-digit numbers can you make using 12 beads?

3 Four children have four different drinks.
Abby would prefer lemonade or blackcurrant.
Bilal would prefer cola.
Carol would prefer cola or orange.
Dan would prefer cola, lemonade or orange?
Who should have each drink?

B

1

H   T   U

898 can be made on an abacus using exactly 25 beads.
How many different 3-digit numbers can be made on an abacus using exactly:
a)   25 beads
b)   24 beads?

2 Five girls will each write one of five pages for the Class 6 Magazine.
Amber would prefer to write the news page or sports page.
Belle would prefer to write the sports page.
Cherry would prefer the sports page or puzzle page.
Dani would prefer the news page, the fashion page or the interview page.
Emma would prefer the fashion or the puzzle page.
Which girl should write each page?

C

1

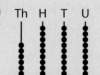

Th H   T   U

6999 can be made on an abacus using exactly 33 beads.
How many different 4-digit numbers can be made on an abacus using exactly:
a)   33 beads
b)   32 beads?

2 Six boys are camping. They decide they will each have one of six jobs.
Ayub prefers to wash up or put up the tent.
Ben prefers to collect firewood or tidy the site.
Carl prefers to cook or put up the tent.
Derek prefers to wash up or tidy the site.
Ewan prefers to cook, collect firewood or go shopping.
Finn would prefer to tidy the site.
Which boy should have each job?

I can write a formula for converting one currency to another.

A

A formula for the number of wheels *w* on *b* bicycles is

$$w = 2b$$

Write a formula for the number of:

1. wheels *w* on *t* tricycles
2. wheels *w* on *c* cars
3. skis *s* for *p* people
4. hours *h* in *d* days
5. minutes *m* in *h* hours
6. years *y* in *c* centuries
7. ferry crossings *c* in *d* days if the ferry makes 4 crossings per day
8. words *w* typed in *m* minutes if the typist's rate is 80 words per minute
9. heart beats *b* in *m* minutes if the pulse rate is 68
10. metres *m* run in *ℓ* laps if one lap is 400 m.

Train tickets cost £6 for an adult and £3 for children. What is the cost *c* for:

11. 4 adults and *g* girls
12. *a* adults and 3 children
13. *a* adults and *b* boys
14. *m* men, 3 women, 2 boys and *g* girls?

B

EXCHANGE RATES
£1 buys:

Danish kroner	11
Euros	1·4
Japanese yen	233
Maltese lira	0·6
Mexican pesos	20
S. African rand	13·3
Swiss francs	2·4
US dollars	1·9

1. Write a formula for exchanging £*x* for each of the above currencies.
   e.g. £*x* = 11*x* kroner

2. Use your formulae to work out how much of each currency could be bought for:
   a) £10
   b) £100
   c) £500.

3. Exchange rates change. Research the current rates in a newspaper or go to www.xe.net/ucc Write each of the current exchange rates as a formula.

4. Investigate exchange rates for other currencies.

C

£1 buys 11 Danish kroner.

1. Use a calculator to work out how much 1 kroner would buy in pounds. Round the amount to the nearest 1p.

2. Write a formula for converting *k* kroner to pounds.

3. Write a formula for converting *x* units of each of the currencies listed in Section B to pounds. Use the exchange rates in Section B or the current rates from a newspaper or the internet.

Use your formulae to find how many pounds you could buy for:

4. 60 Euros
5. 300 Danish kroner
6. 4000 pesos
7. 80 Maltese lira
8. 450 francs
9. 10 000 rand
10. one million yen
11. 68 US dollars.

12. Write a formula for converting *x* Euros to US dollars.

I can use tests of divisibility to check results and to find the prime factors of whole numbers.

Whole numbers are divisible by:
2 if the last digit is even
3 if sum of the digits is divisible by 3
4 if the last 2 digits are divisible by 4
5 if the last digit is 0 or 5
6 if the number is even and divisible by 3
8 if the last 3 digits are divisible by 4
9 if the sum of the digits is divisible by 9.

A factor which is also a prime number is a prime factor. The prime factors of a number can be found using a factor tree.

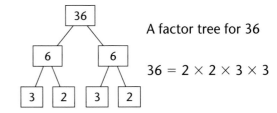

A factor tree for 36

$36 = 2 \times 2 \times 3 \times 3$

A

Write True or False

1. 6000 is divisible by 2.
2. 154 is divisible by 5.
3. 222 is divisible by 4.
4. 25 is divisible by 10.
5. 285 is divisible by 2.
6. 160 is divisible by 5.
7. 270 is divisible by 10.
8. 332 is divisible by 4

Copy and complete the prime factors.

9. $21 = \boxed{} \times 3$
10. $12 = 2 \times 2 \times \boxed{}$
11. $15 = 3 \times \boxed{}$
12. $28 = \boxed{} \times 2 \times 2$
13. $20 = \boxed{} \times \boxed{} \times 5$
14. $16 = 2 \times 2 \times \boxed{} \times \boxed{}$
15. $18 = 3 \times \boxed{} \times \boxed{}$
16. $66 = 2 \times \boxed{} \times \boxed{}$

B

Write True or False

1. 353 is divisible by 3.
2. 48 is divisible by 4.
3. 1458 is divisible by 9.
4. 158 is divisible by 6.
5. 1056 is divisible by 8.
6. 1763 is divisible by 9.
7. 885 is divisible by 3.
8. 376 is divisible by 4.
9. 474 is divisible by 6.
10. 2148 is divisible by 8.
11. 182 is divisible by 4.
12. 798 is divisible by 3.

Use a factor tree to find all the prime factors of:

13. 30
14. 44
15. 51
16. 36
17. 99
18. 38
19. 70
20. 32

C

1. Copy and complete the table.

No.	DIVISIBLE BY					
	3	4	5	6	8	9
336	✓	✓	✗			
740	✗					
675						
207						
168						
825						
780						
344						
432						
552						

Find the missing digits.

2. $\boxed{}25 \div 5 = 6\boxed{}$
3. $\boxed{}32 \div 4 = 8\boxed{}$
4. $2\boxed{}9 \div 9 = \boxed{}1$
5. $4\boxed{}1 \div 3 = 15\boxed{}$
6. $\boxed{}12 \div 8 = 6\boxed{}$
7. $41\boxed{} \div 6 = \boxed{}\boxed{}$
8. $756 \div \boxed{} = 8\boxed{}$

I can find examples to match general statements and solve problems and puzzles.

Examples

Find three examples that match each statement.

1 When you add two odd numbers, the answer is an even number.

$5 + 11 = 16$

$7 + 3 = 10$

$99 + 25 = 124$

2 A multiple of 16 is also a multiple of 8.

$48 = 3 \times 16$ and $48 = 6 \times 8$

$80 = 5 \times 16$ and $80 = 10 \times 8$

$320 = 20 \times 16$ and $320 = 40 \times 8$

A

Find these examples that match each statement.

1 The sum of three consecutive numbers is three times the middle number.

2 A multiple of 9 is also a multiple of 3.

3 Multiplying a decimal number by 100 moves every digit two places to the left.

4 The product of two even numbers is always even.

5 I think of a number, double it and add 6. The answer is 42. What is my number?

Copy and complete.

6 $\boxed{} \div 3 + 2 = 8$

7 $\boxed{} \times 4 - 4 = 28$

8 $\boxed{} \div 5 - 2 = 6$

9 $\boxed{} \times 8 + 7 = 55$

B

Find four examples that match each statement.

1 The sum of four consecutive numbers is double the sum of the middle pair of numbers.

2 A multiple of 12 is also a multiple of 6.

3 Dividing a whole number by 0·5 makes the number twice as big.

4 The product of two or more odd numbers is always odd.

5 I think of a number, multiply by 7 and subtract 13. The answer is 64. What is my number?

Copy and complete.

6 $(\boxed{} - 12) \times 5 = 60$

7 $(\boxed{} + 8) \times 3 = 99$

8 $(\boxed{} - 16) \div 6 = 6$

9 $(\boxed{} + 23) \div 4 = 16$

C

Find four examples that match each statement.

1 The sum of five consecutive numbers is five times the middle number.

2 A multiple of 18 is also a multiple of 3.

3 Dividing a number by 0·1 makes the number ten times as big.

4 The product of any combination of odd and even numbers is always even.

5 I think of a number, add 23 and find one seventh. The answer is 14. What is my number?

Copy and complete.

6 $16 + (240 \div \boxed{}) = 46$

7 $76 + (6 \times \boxed{}) = 130$

8 $\boxed{} - (72 \div 12) = 48$

9 $\boxed{} - (16 \times 7) = 88$

I can classify 3-D shapes according to their properties including recognising parallel and perpendicular faces and edges of shapes with straight edges.

CURVED EDGES
These shapes have curved edges.
cone
cylinder
hemisphere
sphere

cylinder

STRAIGHT EDGES
A shape with straight edges is called a polyhedron.

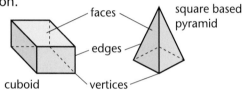

faces
edges
vertices
cuboid
square based pyramid

REGULAR POLYHEDRA
Regular polyhedra have faces which are identical.
cube
regular octahedron
regular tetrahedron

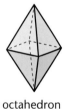

octahedron

PRISMS
A prism is a polyhedron with two identical end faces and the same cross section throughout its length.

Example

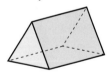

triangular based prism

PARALLEL AND PERPENDICULAR FACES/EDGES
Parallel and perpendicular faces and edges can be identified by placing one face of a shape on a flat surface.

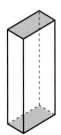

Horizontal faces and edges are parallel to the faces/edges on the flat surface.

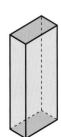

Vertical faces and edges are perpendicular to the faces/edges on the flat surface.

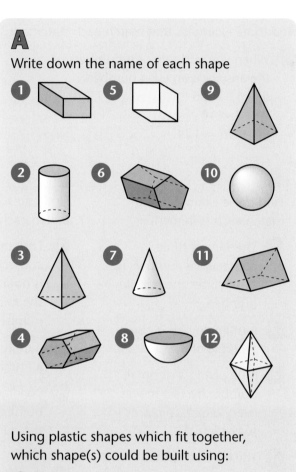

A

Write down the name of each shape

1   5   9

2   6   10

3   7   11

4   8   12

Using plastic shapes which fit together, which shape(s) could be built using:

13 squares only

14 triangles only

15 triangles and rectangles only

16 triangles and squares only?

17 Copy and complete this sentence.
A triangular based prism has ☐ identical triangular end faces and 3 identical ☐ faces.

18 Write a similar sentence for each of the other four prisms in the above diagrams.

B

1 Copy and complete this table showing the features of eight different 3-D shapes.

Name	Faces	Edges	Vertices
		9	
	8		6
cuboid			
			12
		8	
	6		
			10
		6	

2 Look at your table. Describe how, for all the shapes, the number of edges relates to the number of faces plus the number of vertices.

3 A shape has 12 faces and 20 vertices.
  a) How many edges does it have?
  b) It is a prism. Describe its end face.

4 Which of the shapes in your table have:
  a) faces with perpendicular edges
  b) faces with parallel edges
  c) no face with a parallel or perpendicular edge?

5 Work out how many pairs of parallel faces there are in each of the eight shapes in your table.

6 Work out how many pairs of perpendicular faces there are in each of the eight shapes in your table.

7 Which shape has no face with a pair of parallel or perpendicular edges but has parallel and perpendicular edges in the shape?

C

1 This square based pyramid has been cut in a plane parallel to its base.

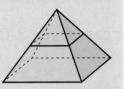

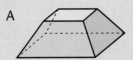 A   B

  a) Describe the faces of shape A.
  b) Name shape B.

Visualise the two shapes made by cutting the following shapes through in the plane shown. For each of the two shapes made either:

a) name the shape

or

b) describe its faces.

2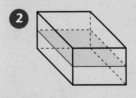

6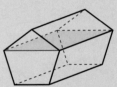

3

7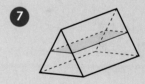

4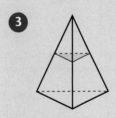

8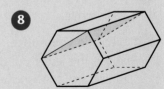

5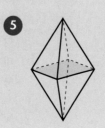

9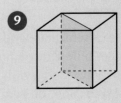

I can make 3-D shapes and draw 2-D shapes with accuracy.

A

1 Copy this net onto squared paper. Cut it out and fold it to make an open cube.

2 Make four different nets that make a closed cube.

3 Make a net for this open cuboid.

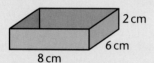

2 cm
6 cm
8 cm

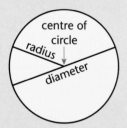

centre of circle
radius
diameter

4 Draw circles with a radius of:

a) 4 cm **b)** 3 cm **c)** 5 cm

5 Measure the diameter of each circle.

6 What do you notice about the length of the radius and the length of the diameter of each circle?

7 Use a set square and ruler only. Draw a right-angled triangle with shorter sides of 3 cm and 4.5 cm.

B

1 Make open cubes with a side of:

a) 1.5 cm

b) 2 cm

c) 2.5 cm.

Do they fit when you make a set of nesting boxes?

2 Make a net for:

a) a triangular based prism with a length of 5 cm and end edges of 3 cm

b) a square based pyramid with a base area of 16 cm² and a height of 4 cm.

3 Write a formula for the diameter (d) of a circle with r radius.

4 Draw a set of circles all having the same centre with diameters of 3, 4, 5 and 6 cm.

5 Draw a similar set of circles with even smaller gaps between them.

6 Use a ruler and a protractor only. Draw:

a) a regular hexagon with 3.6 cm sides

b) an isosceles triangle with two angles of 67° and a shortest side of 2.8 cm.

C

1 Make a set of nesting pyramids.

2 Make a net for:

a) an octahedron with 4 cm edges

b) an hexagonal based prism with a length of 6 cm and 2 cm end edges.

(Using triangular paper may help you design your net.)

3 Construct these patterns.

5 cm   7.6 cm

4 Use a ruler and a protractor only. Construct:

a) a right-angled triangle with a 40° angle and a shortest side of 4.7 cm

b) a parallelogram with sides of 2.3 cm and 5.2 cm and angles of 53° and 127°.

c) a regular pentagon with sides of 2.7 cm

d) an isosceles triangle with one angle of 46° and 2 sides of 3.9 cm.

5 Make up your own compass patterns.

I can read scales accurately and compare readings from different scales.

A

For each scale work out the measurement shown by each arrow.

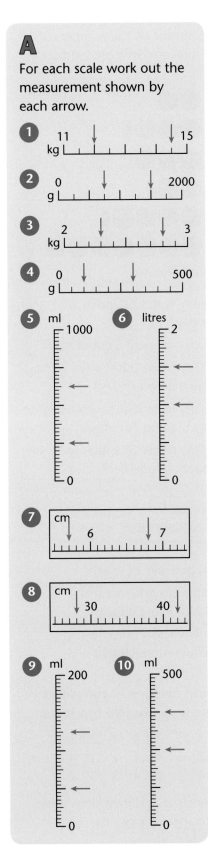

B

Match the measurements shown by X and Y to the equivalent measurements on the second scale.

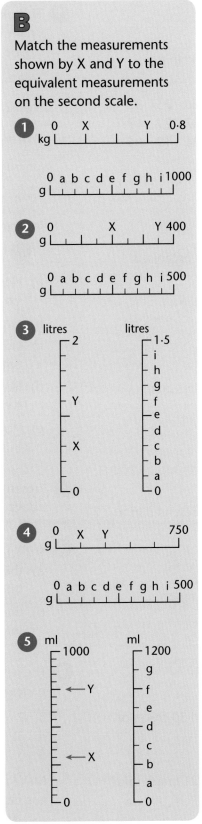

C

Match the measurements shown by X and Y to the equivalent measurements on the second scale.

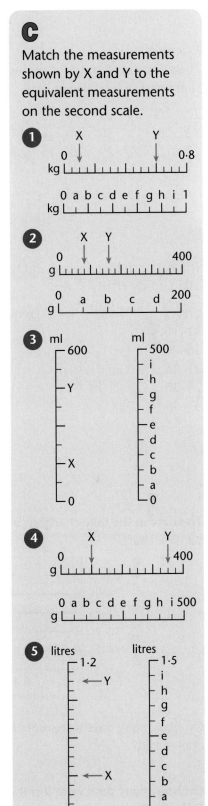

I can draw and interpret bar-line charts and pictograms.

Example

The numbers of crates of apples sold in a supermarket each day in June.

27 20 31 23 18 29 14 26 25 33
22 28 13 30 24 31 27 27 29 17
27 16 32 29 23 15 28 24 19 26

The data can be grouped and then organised using a tally chart.

Crates	Tally	Frequency
11–15	|||	3
16–20	|||||	5
21–25	||||| ||	7
26–30	||||| |||||		11
31–35	||||	4

The data in the tally chart can be presented in a bar-line chart.

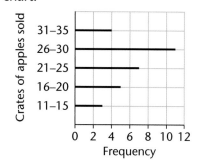

On how many days were more than 30 crates of apples sold?
4

On how many days were less than 21 crates sold?
8 (5 plus 3)

A

1 This pictogram shows the numbers of crates of apples sold in a greengrocer's in one week.

Monday 🍎🍎

Tuesday 🍎🍎🍎◗

Wednesday 🍎🍎🍎

Thursday 🍎🍎◗

Friday 🍎🍎🍎🍎◗

Saturday 🍎🍎🍎🍎🍎🍎🍎

🍎 represents 2 crates

a) How many crates of apples were sold on Tuesday?

b) On which day were 5 crates sold?

c) How many more crates were sold on Saturday than on Friday?

d) How many fewer crates were sold on Monday than on Tuesday?

e) How many crates of apples were sold in the week altogether?

2 Present the data from the pictogram above in a bar-line chart.

3 Write down one way in which:

a) the pictogram presents the information more clearly

b) the bar-line chart presents the information more clearly.

4 The lengths in numbers of completed pages of the stories written by Class 6.

3 2 4 3 5 3 4 4 2 3
4 3 5 2 3 4 1 2 3 4
5 3 1 4 3 2 4 5 3 2

Make a tally chart and then draw a bar-line chart to show the results.

B

1 This bar-line chart shows the numbers of ice creams sold by a cafe in one week.

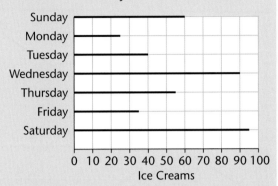

a) How many ice creams were sold on Monday?

b) On which day were 55 ice creams sold?

c) How many more ice creams were sold on Saturday than on Friday?

d) Why do you think more ice creams were sold on Wednesday than on Tuesday?

e) How many ice creams were sold in the week altogether?

f) What was the range of the numbers of ice creams sold?

2 The numbers of fish caught by 40 anglers in a competition.

```
 5   8  17   6  13   6   9  22   7  12
19   9   3  11   8   4  16   8  15  10
13   8  21   7   2  14   8  20   6   4
 8  15   5  18  10   5  23   9  11  16
```

a) What number of fish caught was the mode?

b) What was the largest number of fish caught?

c) What was the smallest number of fish caught?

d) What was the range of numbers of fish caught?

e) Make a tally chart and then present the results in a bar-line chart.

C

1 This bar-line chart shows the numbers of points scored by a basketball team in all their games in three years.

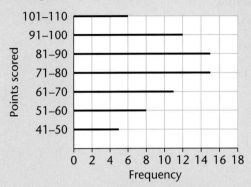

a) In how many games did the team score more than 80 points?

b) In how many games did the team score 70 points or less?

c) How many games were played in the three years?

d) In what proportion of the games did the team score more than 90 points?

e) In what proportion of the games did the team score 70 points or less?

2 The times in minutes when goals were scored in 10 Premiership matches are shown:

```
36  87  53   7  73  28  85  64  43  78
71  15  80  59  83  45  90  21  84  52
60  90  41  82  65  11  48  76  38  69
```

a) Group the data in six 15 minute intervals.

b) Make a tally chart and present the results in a bar-line chart.

3 What proportion of the goals were scored in:

a) the second half

b) the last third?

4 What might explain this uneven distribution. Use the football results published in newspapers to investigate further.

I can use a conversion graph.

Example

This graph converts miles into kilometres.

20 miles converts to 32 km.

64 km converts to 40 miles.

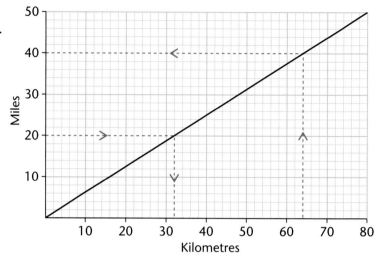

A

The rupee is the currency used in India.
The graph converts rupees into pounds.

1 Convert into pounds:

   a) 280 rupees   **d)** 660 rupees

   b) 420 rupees   **e)** 380 rupees

   c) 600 rupees   **f)** 40 rupees.

2 Convert into rupees:

   a) £8·00   **d)** £7·40

   b) £4·60   **e)** £2·00

   c) £10·00   **f)** £6·60.

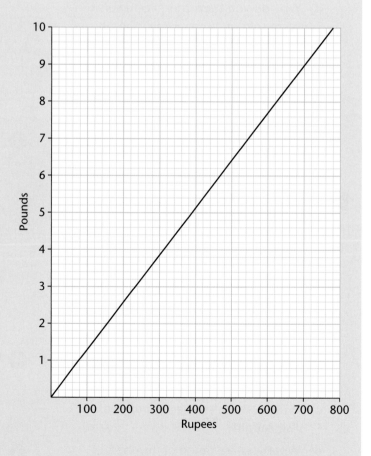

3 On holiday in India, Stanley bought
snake charming lessons worth 9 pounds.
How much did he pay in rupees?

B

This graph converts litres to gallons.

1 Convert to the nearest tenth of a gallon:

a) 18 litres   d) 26 litres

b) 10 litres   e) 36 litres

c) 32 litres   f) 4 litres.

2 Convert to the nearest litre:

a) 2 gallons   d) 3·8 gallons

b) 8·2 gallons   e) 10 gallons

c) 6 gallons   f) 0·2 gallons.

3 Sanya drives 140 miles.
She notices her car has used
18 litres of petrol.
How many miles is she
travelling for every gallon
of petrol used?

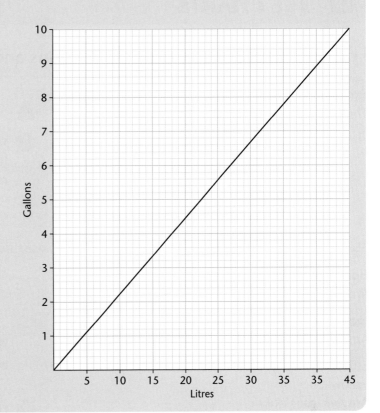

C

1 Use graph paper to draw a graph converting pounds to Euros.

a) Label the horizontal axis in 10s to 100.

b) Label the vertical axis (Euros) in 10s to 140.

c) Plot the points (0, 0) and (100, 140).

d) Join the points with a straight line.

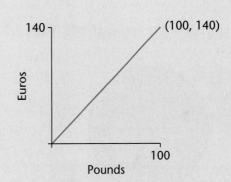

2 Use your graph to convert to Euros:

a) £100   d) £10

b) £30   e) £50

c) £80   f) £62.

3 Use your graph to convert to pounds:

a) €70   d) €126

b) €100   e) €84

c) €28   f) €44.

4 Use graph paper to draw a graph converting test marks out of 60 to percentages.

Label the horizontal axis in 10s to 100. Label the vertical axis in 10s to 60.

Join point (100, 60) to the origin (0, 0).

Use your graph to convert these marks to percentages.

a) 30 out of 60   c) 57 out of 60   e) 51 out of 60

b) 42 out of 60   d) 24 out of 60   f) 33 out of 60.

I can interpret pie charts using fractions and percentages.

Examples

The favourite colours of 80 children.

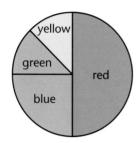

How many children chose red?
Answer *40* (80 ÷ 2)

How many children chose blue?
Answer *20* (80 ÷ 4)

Estimate the proportion of children who chose yellow.
Answer *one eighth*

The 300 members of the audience at a film performance.

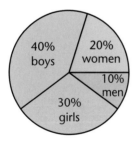

How many men were in the audience?
Answer *30* (10% of 300)

How many girls were in the audience?
Answer *90* (30% of 300)

A

1 The 90 children in Year 6 chose their favourite day of the week. These are the results.

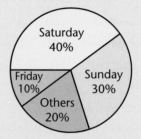

How many children chose:

a) Friday **b)** Saturday **c)** Sunday?

2 The pie chart shows the weather in the 30 days of June.

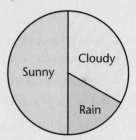

Estimate the number of days which were:

a) sunny **b)** cloudy **c)** wet.

3 The 2500 people at a concert.

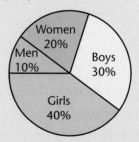

How many of the audience were:

a) men **c)** boys

b) women **d)** girls?

B

The pie charts show how land is used on two farms.

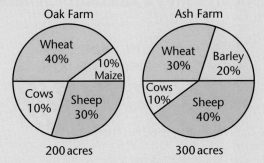

Oak Farm
- Wheat 40%
- 10% Maize
- Cows 10%
- Sheep 30%

200 acres

Ash Farm
- Wheat 30%
- Barley 20%
- Cows 10%
- Sheep 40%

300 acres

1 How many acres of land on Oak Farm are used for:

a) growing maize

b) grazing sheep?

2 How many acres of land on Ash Farm are used for:

a) grazing cattle

b) growing barley?

3 Gina says

More land is used on Oak Farm than on Ash Farm for growing wheat.

Use both charts to explain why this is not correct.

4 The pie charts show the cold drinks chosen by a class of children and the adults accompanying them on a trip.

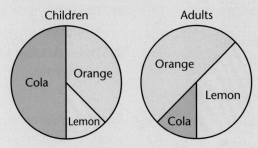

Children
- Cola
- Orange
- Lemon

Adults
- Orange
- Lemon
- Cola

4 children and 4 adults chose lemon.

a) Estimate the size of the class.

b) Estimate the number of adults on the trip.

c) Draw how you think the pie charts would look if tea had been an available choice.

C

The pie charts show how the Turners spent £600 on a week's holiday in England and £1000 on a week's holiday in Spain.

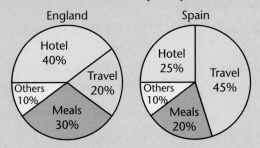

England
- Hotel 40%
- Travel 20%
- Others 10%
- Meals 30%

Spain
- Hotel 25%
- Travel 45%
- Others 10%
- Meals 20%

1 On their English holiday how much did the Turners spend:

a) on travel   b) on meals?

2 On their Spanish holiday how much did the Turners spend on everything apart from their travel costs?

3 Keith says

The hotel cost more in England than in Spain.

Debra disagrees. Who is right? Use both pie charts to explain your answers.

4 Draw how you think the pie charts would look if the Turners took:

a) a 2 week holiday in Spain

b) a one week holiday in Australia.

5 The pie charts show how 570 people travelled from London to Paris, either by air or by rail.

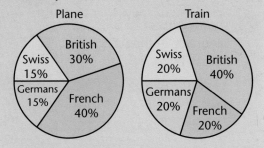

Plane
- British 30%
- Swiss 15%
- Germans 15%
- French 40%

Train
- Swiss 20%
- British 40%
- Germans 20%
- French 20%

33 people from Switzerland went by plane.

a) How many more British people went by train than plane?

b) How many more French people went by plane than train?

I can find the range, mode, median and mean using a calculator where appropriate.

Example	The marks of 10 children in a test.	71% 54% 83% 62% 38% 90% 75% 77% 43% 62%
THE RANGE	The difference between the highest and lowest values.	Highest − Lowest = 90 − 38 The range is 52%.
THE MODE	The most common value.	The mode is 62%. (twice)
THE MEDIAN	The middle value when the numbers are in size order.	The median is 66·5%. (halfway between 62% and 71%)
THE MEAN	The total divided by the number of items in the set.	655 ÷ 10 The mean is 65·5%.

A

Use a calculator if needed. For each of the following sets of data find:

a) the range

b) the mode

c) the median

d) the mean.

1 The numbers of goals scored by a school football team in their 12 matches.

1 3 0 3 1 2
4 1 2 1 0 3

2 The weights in kilograms of the school netball team.

37 31 39 28
41 37 32

3 The weight in kilograms of fish eaten daily by a dolphin.

12·3 16·2 10·8
12·3 13·4

B

Class 6 investigated the forces needed to drag a box across different surfaces. This table shows one group's results.

Test Number	Force needed on:	
	Carpet	Tiles
Test 1	5·6 N	1·4 N
Test 2	7·8 N	1·7 N
Test 3	4·7 N	1·5 N
Test 4	4·8 N	3·7 N
Test 5	5·1 N	1·2 N

1 Find the median and the mean for both sets of data.

2 Explain why the average or typical value for both sets of data is better shown by the median than the mean.

3 Explain why the children tested each material more than once.

C

1 A teacher timed how long seven children took to complete a test. The median time was 11 minutes and the range of times was 6 minutes. Write *Possible* or *Impossible* for each statement.

a) The quickest time was 6 minutes.

b) The slowest time was 18 minutes.

c) The mean time was 8 minutes.

d) Three children took 12 minutes.

2 Thirteen children took a test. Their marks out of 100 were as follows.

64 47 56 52 48 63 72
59 68 35 70 ☐ ☐
The mean mark was 58. The range was 40. What are the two missing marks?

I can use the language of probability to describe the likelihood of an event.

The probability of an event can be placed on a scale.

Examples

1 My next birthday will fall on a Tuesday.

2 You spin a coin and get a tail.

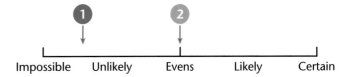

Impossible   Unlikely   Evens   Likely   Certain

A

What is the probability of the arrow pointing at an orange section when each of these spinners stops spinning?

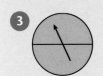

9 Place each probability on a scale like the one above.

10 Draw a spinner with four sections where the probability of the arrow landing on blue is evens, on red is unlikely and on yellow is impossible.

B

Place the probabilities of these events on a scale.

1 You roll a dice and get a 6.

2 Tomorrow will be a sunny day.

3 You spin 2 coins and do not get 2 heads.

4 The next car to pass the school is white.

5 A cat gives birth to puppies.

6 You draw a card from a pack and get an ace.

Kelly's Spinner   Matilda's Spinner

7 Which spinner is more likely to land on:

a) a 4

b) a number greater than 4

c) a number less than 4

d) an even number

e) a prime number?

C

Work out the probability of each event as a fraction. Use that knowledge to place the probabilities accurately on a scale.

You draw a card from a pack and it is:

1 a heart

2 red

3 the Queen of hearts.

The first of the 50 numbered balls in the Lotto Draw is:

4 over 40

5 a multiple of 3

6 not a multiple of 5.

You spin 3 coins and get:

7 3 heads

8 two heads, one tail

9 two tails, one head.

Using this spinner you land on:

10 an odd number

11 an even number.

12 5.

I can suggest suitable units for measurements and I can convert a measurement to an alternative form.

UNITS OF LENGTH

$$km \xrightarrow{\times1000} m \xrightarrow{\times100} cm \xrightarrow{\times10} mm$$
$$km \xleftarrow{\div1000} m \xleftarrow{\div100} cm \xleftarrow{\div10} mm$$

Examples

1 km 320 m = 1320 m = 1·32 km

5 m 47 cm = 547 cm = 5·47 m

2 cm 8 mm = 28 mm = 2·8 cm

UNITS OF MASS

$$kg \xrightarrow{\times1000} g$$
$$kg \xleftarrow{\div1000} g$$

Examples

6 kg 100 g = 6100 g = 6·1 kg

1 kg 270 g = 1270 g = 1·27 kg

0 kg 625 g = 625 g = 0·625 kg

UNITS OF CAPACITY

$$litres \xrightarrow{\times1000} ml$$
$$litres \xleftarrow{\div1000} ml$$

Examples

3 litres 450 ml = 3450 ml = 3·45 litres

8 litres 600 ml = 8600 ml = 8·6 litres

0 litres 35 ml = 35 ml = 0·035 litres

A

Copy and complete.

1. 0 cm 2 mm = ☐ mm = ☐ cm

2. 4 m 63 cm = ☐ cm = ☐ m

3. 5 km 800 m = ☐ m = ☐ km

4. 0 kg 600 g = ☐ g = ☐ kg

5. 5 litres 170 ml = ☐ ml = ☐ litres

6. 7 cm 9 mm = ☐ mm = ☐ cm

7. 0 m 27 cm = ☐ cm = ☐ m

8. 16 km 700 m = ☐ m = ☐ km

9. 1 kg 800 g = ☐ g = ☐ kg

10. 0 litres 290 ml = ☐ ml = ☐ litres

11. 153 mm = ☐ cm ☐ mm = ☐ cm

12. 580 cm = ☐ m ☐ cm = ☐ m

13. 900 m = ☐ km ☐ m = ☐ km

14. 12 040 g = ☐ kg ☐ g = ☐ kg

15. 3400 ml = ☐ litres ☐ ml = ☐ litres

16. 40 mm = ☐ cm ☐ mm = ☐ cm

17. 1924 cm = ☐ m ☐ cm = ☐ m

18. 2350 m = ☐ km ☐ m = ☐ km

19. 7600 g = ☐ kg ☐ g = ☐ kg

20. 2680 ml = ☐ litres ☐ ml = ☐ litres

Suggest a suitable metric unit to measure:

21. the length of a charity walk

22. the weight of an ear ring

23. the length of a necklace

24. the capacity of a medicine bottle

25. the length of a wood lice

26. the weight of a bus

27. the height of the classroom

28. the capacity of a toilet cistern

B

Copy and complete.

1. 19·37 m = ☐ m ☐ cm = ☐ cm
2. 0·62 m = ☐ m ☐ mm = ☐ mm
3. 4·075 km = ☐ km ☐ m = ☐ m
4. 3·6 kg = ☐ kg ☐ g = ☐ g
5. 72·5 litres = ☐ litres ☐ ml = ☐ ml
6. 2·06 m = ☐ cm = ☐ m ☐ cm
7. 0·08 m = ☐ mm = ☐ m ☐ mm
8. 0·136 km = ☐ m = ☐ km ☐ m
9. 0·045 kg = ☐ g = ☐ kg ☐ g
10. 6·185 litres = ☐ ml = ☐ litres ☐ ml
11. 4 cm = ☐ m ☐ cm = ☐ m
12. 975 mm = ☐ m ☐ mm = ☐ m
13. 9 m = ☐ km ☐ m = ☐ km
14. 72 050 g = ☐ kg ☐ g = ☐ kg
15. 390 ml = ☐ litres ☐ ml = ☐ litres
16. 8150 cm = ☐ m = ☐ m ☐ cm
17. 31 400 mm = ☐ m = ☐ m ☐ mm
18. 52 830 m = ☐ km = ☐ km ☐ m
19. 185 g = ☐ kg = ☐ kg ☐ g
20. 5 ml = ☐ litres = ☐ litres ☐ ml

Suggest a suitable metric unit to measure:

21. the mass of a dining table
22. the area of the playground
23. the capacity of a syringe
24. the width of a watch strap
25. the mass of a sparrow
26. the length of the River Nile
27. the capacity of a horse trough
28. the length of a watch strap

C

Copy and complete each sentence by choosing the best estimate.

1. The height of Mount Everest is (0·89 km, 8·9 km, 0·089 km).
2. The thickness of an exercise book is (0·5 cm, 0·05 cm, 0·05 m).
3. A bed is (200 mm, 2000 mm, 20 000 mm) long.
4. The length of a pair of scissors is (0·13 m, 0·013 m, 13 mm).
5. A tablespoon has a capacity of (0·001 litres, 0·01 litres, 0·1 litres).
6. A vase has a capacity of (6 ml, 60 ml, 600 ml).
7. Nikki is 10. She has a mass of about (400 g, 4000 g, 40 000 g).
8. A robin weighs about (2 g, 20 g, 200 g).

Arrange these measurements in ascending order.

9. 6600 ml   9 litres   960 ml   6·9 litres
10. 4020 ml   2·24 litres   2400 ml   4·2 litres
11. 580 g   0·8 kg   850 g   0·5 kg
12. 1·7 kg   1177 g   1·17 kg   1117 g
13. 5005 mm   5·5 m   555 cm   0·005 km
14. 2700 m   2·27 km   0·772 km   77 000 cm
15. 0·808 m   888 mm   88 cm   0·008 km
16. 334 cm   3·4 m   0·033 km   3334 mm

I can convert imperial units to their approximate metric equivalents and vice versa.

These are the most commonly used imperial units and their metric equivalents.
(The sign '≈' means 'is approximately equal to'.)

LENGTH
1 inch ≈ 2·5 cm
1 foot ≈ 30 cm
1 yard ≈ 90 cm
1 mile ≈ 1·6 km
8 km ≈ 5 miles

MASS
1 ounce ≈ 30 g
1 kg ≈ 2·2 pounds

CAPACITY
1 pint ≈ 0·6 litres
1 gallon ≈ 4·5 litres

A

Which imperial unit would you use to measure:

1. a garden's length
2. a bag of sugar's weight
3. a pencil's length
4. a bowl's capacity
5. a country's length
6. the weight of an egg
7. a door's height
8. a pond's capacity?

Copy and complete.

9. 10 inches ≈ ☐ cm
10. 2 feet ≈ ☐ cm
11. 10 yards ≈ ☐ m
12. 2 miles ≈ ☐ km

13. 3 ounces ≈ ☐ g
14. 4·4 pounds ≈ ☐ kg
15. 4 pints ≈ ☐ litres
16. 2 gallons ≈ ☐ litres

17. 150 cm ≈ ☐ feet
18. 4 km ≈ ☐ miles
19. 3 kg ≈ ☐ pounds
20. 1·2 litres ≈ ☐ pints

B

Choose the best estimate.

1. a pen
   6, 9 or 12 inches
2. a bath
   1, 10 or 100 gallons
3. a man's weight
   2, 20 or 200 pounds
4. a tree's height
   6, 60 or 600 feet

Copy and complete.

5. 4 inches ≈ ☐ cm
6. 6 feet ≈ ☐ m
7. 5 yards ≈ ☐ m
8. 100 miles ≈ ☐ km

9. 4 ounces ≈ ☐ g
10. 22 pounds ≈ ☐ kg
11. 5 pints ≈ ☐ litres
12. 20 gallons ≈ ☐ litres

13. 100 cm ≈ ☐ inches
14. 80 km ≈ ☐ miles
15. 5 kg ≈ ☐ pounds
16. 12 litres ≈ ☐ pints

C

Copy and complete by putting > or < in the box.

1. 9 miles ☐ 14 km
2. 17 ounces ☐ 0·5 kg
3. 7 yards ☐ 6·5 m
4. 8 gallons ☐ 35 litres

5. 11 inches ☐ 29 cm
6. 18 pounds ☐ 8 kg
7. 12 miles ☐ 20 km
8. 15 yards ☐ 14 m

9. 14 feet ☐ 4·1 m
10. 5 inches ☐ 12 cm
11. 4 pints ☐ 2·2 litres
12. 12 gallons ☐ 55 litres

13. To the nearest pound, how many pounds are there in:
    a) 100 kg c) 5 kg
    b) 14 kg d) 26 kg?

14. To the nearest tenth of a gallon, how many gallons are there in:
    a) 9 litres c) 14 litres
    b) 5 litres d) 18 litres?

I can read scales accurately.

For each of the scales work out:

a) the measurement indicated by each of the arrows

b) the difference between the two arrows.

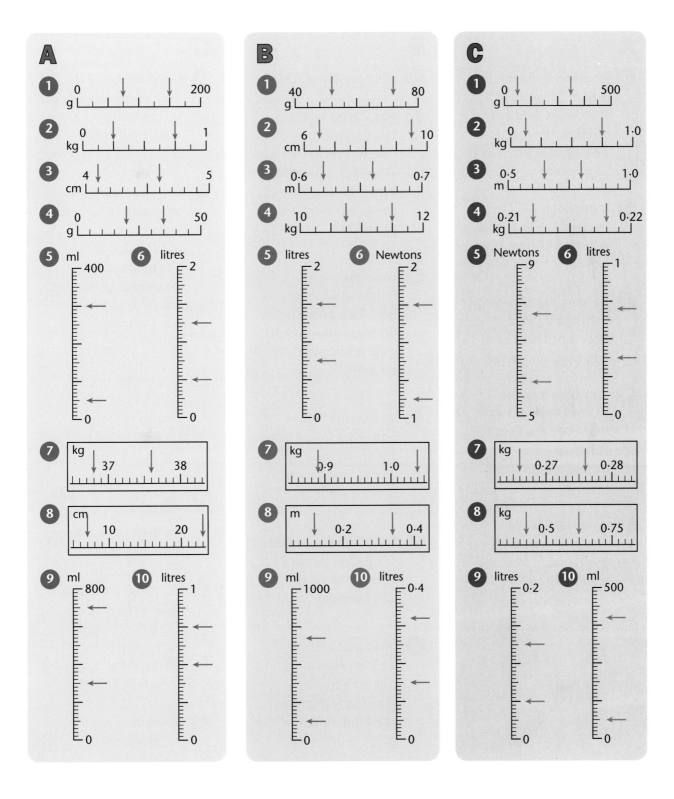

I can solve problems involving measures.

Example

A box holding 65 matches weighs 20 g.
The box weighs 8·3 g.
What is the weight of one match?

20 g − 8·3 g = 11·7 g
11·7 g ÷ 65 = 0·18 g
One match weighs 0·18 g.

A

1. Jonathan walks for 2·6 km. He rests and then walks a further 1400 m. How far does he walk altogether in kilometres?

2. A can holds 0·2 litres of cycle oil. 26 ml is used. A further 47 ml is used. How much oil is left?

3. Six identical eggs weigh 0·48 kg altogether. How much does each egg weigh in grams?

4. Sally buys four shelves 65 cm long and two shelves 75 cm long. How many metres of shelving does this provide?

5. How many 80 ml scoops of ice cream can be taken from five 2 litre tubs?

B

1. What is 28% of £335?

2. Mrs. Gregg receives two parcels. One weighs 380 g. The other is twice as heavy. What is their combined weight in kilograms?

3. There are twelve bottles of wine in a box. Each bottle holds 0·7 litres. How much wine is there in three boxes?

4. Seema cuts 0·68 m from 2 metres of string. She then cuts a further 35 cm. How much string is left?

5. The 300 rubber bands in a packet weigh 24 g. What is the weight of 120 bands?

6. Dried fruit costs £1·50 for 1 kg. Petra buys a bag for 90p. How many grams of dried fruit does she buy?

C

1. Fish costs £6·40 for 1 kg. Boris buys 225 g. He pays with a £5 note. How much change will he receive?

2. The maximum temperature recorded in one year in London was 28·4°C. The range of the temperatures recorded was 37·6°C. What was the minimum temperature?

3. A carpenter needs eighty-eight 40 cm lengths of wood. How many 3·6 m planks will he need?

4. Each tea bag contains 2·5 g of tea. How many tea bags can be made from 4 kg of tea?

5. 15 289 people visit a castle in July. £55 040.40 is raised by the sale of entrance tickets. What is the cost of each ticket?

6. How many minutes are there in June?

I can solve problems involving area and perimeter.

Example
Find the area of
this L-shaped garden.

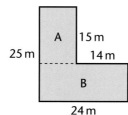

25 m

A 15 m
14 m

B

24 m

Area of A = (15 × 10) m² = 150 m²
Area of B = (24 × 10) m² = 240 m²
Area of garden = (240 + 150) m² = 390 m²

A

1. Copy and complete the table showing the length, width, perimeter and area of rectangles.

L	W	P	A
cm	cm	cm	cm²
6	5		
7	4		
10			50
9		30	

Use 1 cm² paper.

2. Draw two different rectangles each with an area of 30 cm². Work out the perimeters.

3. Draw two different rectangles each with a perimeter of 30 cm. Work out the areas.

4. Use 1 cm² paper. Draw as many shapes as you can with an area of 2 cm².

Example

B

1. Find the area of:
   a) the rectangles
   b) the triangles.

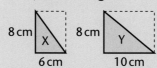

8 cm   X   8 cm   Y
6 cm   10 cm

2. Work out the smallest area of paper needed to cover this cuboid.

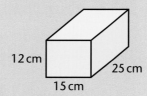

12 cm
25 cm
15 cm

3. A rectangular playground is 25 metres wide. It has an area of 1000 m². Work out the perimeter.

A room measures 6 m by 4 m.

4. What will it cost to cover the floor with carpet costing £18 per square metre?

5. How many 25 cm by 25 cm tiles would be needed to cover the floor?

C

1. Work out the area of each right-angled triangle.

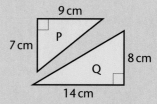

9 cm
7 cm   P
                8 cm
        Q
14 cm

2. Use 1 cm² paper. Draw as many shapes with an area of 3 cm² as you can.

3. Work out the measurements of this cuboid.

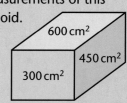

600 cm²
450 cm²
300 cm²

4. A garden has a 1 m wide path around a patio and lawn.

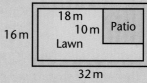

16 m

18 m
10 m   Patio
Lawn

32 m

Work out
   a) the area of the path
   b) the area of the lawn
   c) the perimeter of the path
   d) the number of 50 cm by 50 cm tiles needed to cover the patio.

I can find the missing angles in a triangle, on a straight line and around a point.

Examples

- ANGLES ON A STRAIGHT LINE
  The sum of the angles on a straight line is 180°.

$$x + 57° = 180°$$
$$x = 123°$$

- ANGLES AT A POINT
  A whole turn is 360°.

$$y + 80° = 360°$$
$$y = 280°$$

- ANGLES IN A TRIANGLE
  The sum of the angles in a triangle is 180°.

$$z + 110° = 180°$$
$$z = 70°$$

A

Find the angles marked with letters.

1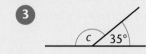

3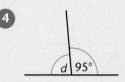

2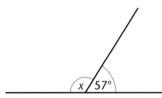

4

5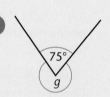

7

6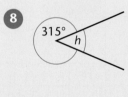

8

9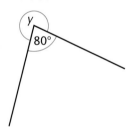

11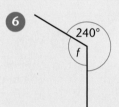

10

12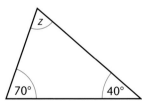

How many degrees is the clockwise turn from:

13 N to NE   **17** S to E

14 W to N   **18** SE to NW

15 NE to S   **19** E to NE

16 NW to S   **20** SW to N?

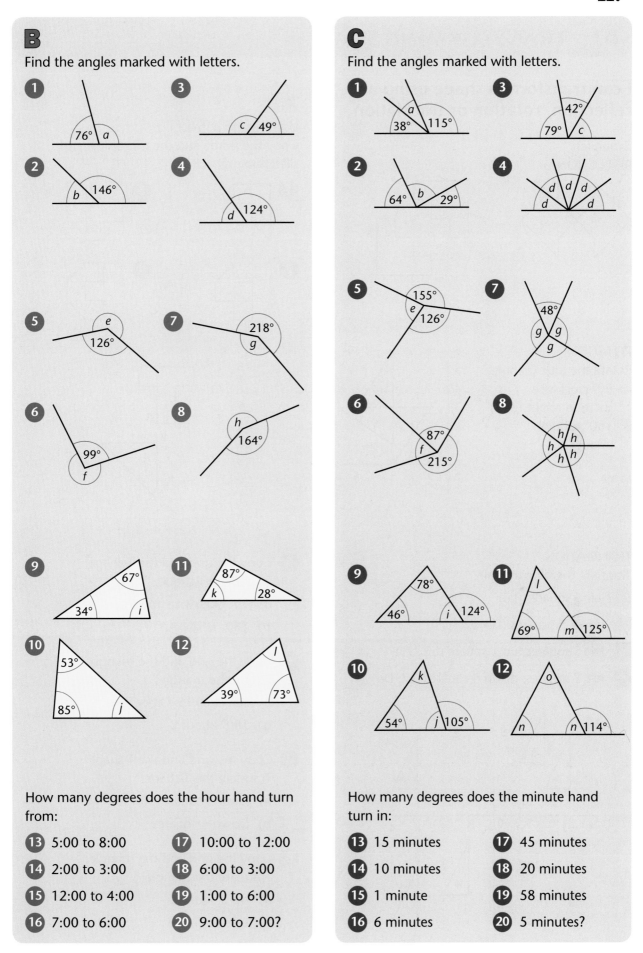

B

Find the angles marked with letters.

1 76° a

2 b 146°

3 c 49°

4 d 124°

5 e 126°

7 218° g

6 99° f

8 h 164°

9 67° 34° i

11 87° k 28°

10 53° 85° j

12 l 39° 73°

How many degrees does the hour hand turn from:

13 5:00 to 8:00

14 2:00 to 3:00

15 12:00 to 4:00

16 7:00 to 6:00

17 10:00 to 12:00

18 6:00 to 3:00

19 1:00 to 6:00

20 9:00 to 7:00?

C

Find the angles marked with letters.

1 a 38° 115°

2 64° b 29°

3 42° 79° c

4 d d d d d

5 155° e 126°

7 48° g g g

6 87° f 215°

8 h h h h

9 78° 46° i 124°

11 l 69° m 125°

10 k 54° j 105°

12 o n n 114°

How many degrees does the minute hand turn in:

13 15 minutes

14 10 minutes

15 1 minute

16 6 minutes

17 45 minutes

18 20 minutes

19 58 minutes

20 5 minutes?

I can transform a shape using a reflection, rotation or translation.

Examples
REFLECTION

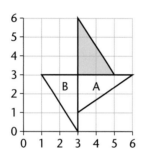

ROTATION
Rotate the blue triangle:

A: 90° clockwise
rotation about (3, 3)

B: 180° rotation
about (3, 3)

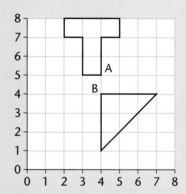

TRANSLATION
Translate the blue triangle:

1 left 6 squares (L6)

2 down 5 squares (D5)

3 left 5 squares, up 1 square (L5, U1)

4 left 2 squares, down 4 squares (L2, D4)

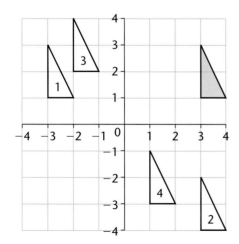

A

Use squared paper.
Copy the shape and the mirror line and
sketch the reflection.

1 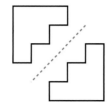   3

2   4

5 Copy the grid and the T-shape.
Rotate the T-shape:

a) 90° clockwise about A

b) 180° about A.

6 Copy the grid and the triangle.
Rotate the triangle:

a) 90° clockwise about B

b) 180° about B.

7 Copy the grid and the T-shape.
Translate the T-shape:

a) Right 3 squares

b) Down 4 squares

8 Copy the grid and the triangle.
Translate the triangle:

a) Up 3 squares

b) Left 4 squares

B

Use squared paper.
Copy the shape and the mirror line and sketch the reflection.

1

3

2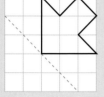

4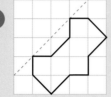

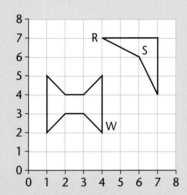

5 Copy the grid and the quadrilateral.
Rotate the quadrilateral:

  a) 90° clockwise about R(4, 7)

  b) 180° about S(6, 6)

6 Copy the grid and the octagon.
Rotate the octagon:

  a) 90° clockwise about W(4, 2)

  b) 90° about the centre of the shape.

7 Copy the grid and the quadrilateral.
Translate the quadrilateral:

  a) L4 U1   **b)** R1 D4   **c)** L3 D3

8 Copy the grid and the octagon.
Translate the octagon:

  a) R3 U2   **b)** L1 U3   **c)** R4 D1

C

Use squared paper.
Copy the shape and the mirror line and sketch the reflection.

1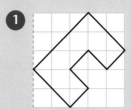

3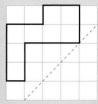

2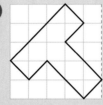

4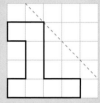

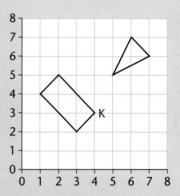

5 Copy the grid and the rectangle.
Rotate the rectangle:

  a) 90° clockwise about K(4, 3)

  b) 90° about the centre of the shape.

6 Copy the grid and the triangle.
Rotate the triangle:

  a) 90° clockwise about (4, 4)

  b) 180° clockwise about (4, 4).

7 Copy the grid and the triangle.
Translate the triangle:

  a) L3 U1   **b)** R1 D4   **c)** L2 D3

8 Copy the grid and the rectangle.
Translate the rectangle:

  a) R3 D2   **b)** L1 U3   **c)** R4 U2

I can estimate the size of angles and use a protractor to measure them.

A

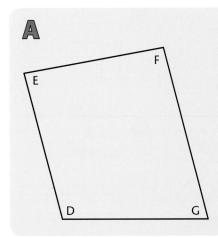

1 Estimate the size of each angle in the quadrilateral to the nearest 5°.

2 Measure the angles.

3 Find the size of each angle in the following regular polygons.

   a) an equilateral triangle

   b) a square

   c) a regular hexagon

B

1 Copy and complete this table for regular polygons.

SHAPE	SIDES	INTERNAL ANGLE	SUM OF ANGLES
equilateral triangle	3		
	4		
	5		
	6		
regular heptagon	7	128·71°	900°
	8		

REGULAR HEPTAGON

Internal angle = 128·71°

128·71° × 7 = 900°

2 Use the pattern in your table to work out the internal angle of:

   a) a regular nonagon (9 sides)

   b) a regular decagon (10 sides)

C

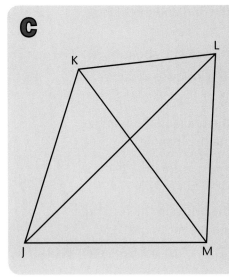

1 Estimate and then measure to the nearest degree the angles of these triangles.

   a) JKL   **c)** JLM

   b) KLM   **d)** JKM

2 Draw three irregular pentagons.
Find the sum of the internal angles.
What do you notice?

3 Investigate the sum of the internal angles of other irregular polygons.

I can work out mental calculations involving fractions, decimals or percentages.

A

1. Take seven tenths from 6.

2. What is one third of a right angle?

3. How many quarters make 5?

4. What is 50% larger than 12?

5. Subtract three quarters from 8.

6. Find one fifth of 30.

7. Add five eighths and two eighths.

8. What is the product of 4 and 0·7?

9. What is the difference between 1·5 and 3·9?

10. Divide 3·6 by 9.

11. Which number is 10 times greater than 2·7?

12. What is 10% of 30?

13. What is half of 7?

14. Which number is 10 times smaller than 0·9?

15. Increase 4·2 by 1·9.

B

1. What is added to 0·57 to make 1?

2. Double 6·8.

3. What is one half of 0·5?

4. What is the cost of a £3 T-shirt if the price is reduced by 20%?

5. Divide 45 by 100.

6. What is three quarters plus one half?

7. Take four tenths from 0·72.

8. Find five eighths of 40.

9. Multiply 0·046 by 100.

10. What is the difference between 2·4 and 0·36?

11. Increase £5·00 by 10%.

12. How many ninths are there in 6?

13. What is one quarter plus nine tenths?

14. Find one fifth of 360°.

15. What is 99 per cent of £10?

C

1. Find seven eighths of 96.

2. What is the product of 5 and 0·37?

3. What is added to 3·74 to make 10?

4. What is one quarter of a right angle?

5. Take six hundredths from 0·541.

6. What is the total of one half, three fifths and two tenths?

7. Which number is 1000 times greater than 0·03?

8. Subtract 0·128 from 2.

9. Find 5% of £300.

10. What is one fifth of 0·7?

11. Increase £2300 by 1%.

12. What is 0·6 multiplied by itself?

13. Find one quarter of 0·1.

14. Add three fifths to 1·73.

15. Find 30% of 240.

I can use a standard written method to add and subtract whole numbers and decimals.

Examples

3248 + 1572   19·56 + 6·247   5728 − 2694   2·58 − 1·743

$$\begin{array}{r} 3248 \\ +1572 \\ \hline 4820 \\ \scriptstyle 1\ 1 \end{array}$$

$$\begin{array}{r} 19{\cdot}56 \\ +\ 6{\cdot}247 \\ \hline 25{\cdot}807 \\ \scriptstyle 1\ \ \ 1 \end{array}$$ Line up the decimal points.

$$\begin{array}{r} 5\overset{6}{\cancel{7}}\overset{1}{2}8 \\ -2694 \\ \hline 3034 \end{array}$$

$$\begin{array}{r} \overset{1}{\cancel{2}}{\cdot}\overset{17}{5}\overset{1}{8}0 \\ -1{\cdot}743 \\ \hline 0{\cdot}837 \end{array}$$ Put in the missing zero.

A

Copy and complete.

1 583 + 249

6 437 − 186

2 659 + 278

7 293 − 175

3 871 + 685

8 359 − 268

4 1654 + 927

9 565 − 437

5 2087 + 359

10 681 − 394

Set out correctly and work out.

11 36·4 + 18·6

12 7·86 + 2·75

13 94·7 + 59·3

14 13·68 + 4·67

15 49·23 + 95·8

16 7·24 − 2·55

17 3·6 − 2·89

18 95·3 − 56·4

19 2·3 − 1·78

20 8·72 − 3·17

B

Copy and complete.

1 4287 + 1946

6 4160 − 2381

2 3649 + 1578

7 6315 − 3678

3 4564 + 2788

8 5873 − 4132

4 6478 + 1957

9 3140 − 2753

5 5895 + 2578

10 7522 − 3947

Set out correctly and work out.

11 43·92 + 46·78

12 2·685 + 5·94

13 41·7 + 28·63

14 72·54 + 4·185

15 8·769 + 9·46

16 41·6 − 23·81

17 63·15 − 36·7

18 8·73 − 4·132

19 75·22 − 39·4

20 31·4 − 27·53

C

Use the above standard method to work out.

1 3486 + 1957

2 12 385 + 7850

3 23 408 + 15 473

4 9748 + 2976

5 5839 + 7794

6 16 512 − 14 675

7 13 747 − 12 968

8 27 934 − 18 157

9 32 158 − 25 389

10 50 361 − 33 596

Set out correctly and work out.

11 17·564 + 39·88

12 47·138 + 4·662

13 867·5 + 39·76

14 25·923 + 5·877

15 56·79 + 7·692

16 24·06 − 17·555

17 375·17 − 29·831

18 46·234 − 38·59

19 248·9 − 188·99

20 31·18 − 24·637

I can multiply two-digit and three-digit numbers by one-digit and two-digit numbers.

Examples

```
  246   Work from the
×   5   right and carry.
 1230
 1 2 3
```

```
   46
×  35
 1380   46 × 30
  230   46 × 5
 1610
    1
```

```
  246
×  35
 7380   246 × 30
 1230   246 × 5
 8610
    1
```

A

Copy and complete.

1
```
  389
×   5
        300 × 5
         80 × 5
          9 × 5
```

2
```
  683
×   7
        600 × 7
         80 × 7
          3 × 7
```

3
```
   49
×  23
        40 × 20
         9 × 20
        40 × 3
         9 × 3
```

4
```
   56
×  34
        50 × 30
         6 × 30
        50 × 4
         6 × 4
```

B

Copy and complete.

1
```
  968
×   3
```

4
```
  392
×   8
```

2
```
  576
×   4
```

5
```
  475
×   6
```

3
```
  758
×   9
```

6
```
  269
×   7
```

Copy and complete.

7
```
  38
×15
```

13
```
  163
×  16
```

8
```
  48
×26
```

14
```
  381
×  25
```

9
```
  83
×37
```

15
```
  258
×  18
```

10
```
  67
×29
```

16
```
  429
×  43
```

11
```
  59
×42
```

17
```
  347
×  28
```

12
```
  74
×34
```

18
```
  439
×  32
```

C

Copy and complete.

1
```
 2763
×   6
```

7
```
  217
×124
```

2
```
 3879
×   4
```

8
```
  531
×245
```

3
```
 2729
×   9
```

9
```
  284
×139
```

4
```
 1681
×   8
```

10
```
  423
×256
```

5
```
 2675
×   7
```

11
```
  336
×194
```

6
```
 4829
×   3
```

12
```
  528
×127
```

13 A book has 184 pages. The mean number of words per page is 317. How many words are there in the book?

14 A film company hires 426 extras to film crowd scenes. They are paid £275 each. What is the total wage bill?

I can divide three-digit numbers by two-digit numbers.

Examples

526 ÷ 22

Estimate

526 ÷ 22

is about

500 ÷ 20

The answer
is about 25.

526
−220 (22 × 10)
$\overset{2\,1}{\cancel{3}06}$
−220 (22 × 10)
86
− 66 (22 × 3)
20

Answer 23 r 20

or

$\overset{4\,1}{\cancel{5}26}$
−440 (22 × 20)
86
− 66 (22 × 3)
20

Answer 23 r 20

A

Work out

1. 172 ÷ 4
2. 147 ÷ 6
3. 251 ÷ 3
4. 131 ÷ 5

5. 257 ÷ 6
6. 268 ÷ 7
7. 206 ÷ 8
8. 553 ÷ 9

9. 228 ÷ 5
10. 385 ÷ 8
11. 381 ÷ 7
12. 234 ÷ 9

13. 437 ÷ 8
14. 855 ÷ 9
15. 201 ÷ 7
16. 664 ÷ 8

B

Work out

1. 217 ÷ 14
2. 660 ÷ 31
3. 602 ÷ 24
4. 686 ÷ 42

5. 900 ÷ 37
6. 841 ÷ 38
7. 586 ÷ 13
8. 640 ÷ 36

9. 634 ÷ 51
10. 970 ÷ 44
11. 956 ÷ 27
12. 746 ÷ 45

13. 581 ÷ 22
14. 830 ÷ 39
15. 630 ÷ 26
16. 999 ÷ 33

17. A florist makes 34 identical bouquets from 476 flowers. How many flowers are there in each bouquet?

18. A tourist exchanges £46 for 828 Swedish kronar. How many kronar would £1 buy?

C

Work out

1. 490 ÷ 23
2. 567 ÷ 15
3. 1176 ÷ 21
4. 1000 ÷ 24
5. 619 ÷ 18
6. 830 ÷ 16

7. 706 ÷ 32
8. 1066 ÷ 26
9. 1421 ÷ 43
10. 774 ÷ 29
11. 982 ÷ 37
12. 1066 ÷ 19

13. There are 32 screws in each bag. How many bags can be filled from 1504 screws?

14. 24 identical crates weigh 864 kg altogether. What is the weight of one crate?

15. Aaron earns £19 656 in a year. How much is he paid each week?

16. One box holds 48 tins. How many boxes are needed for 1104 tins?

I can find equivalent fractions and simplify fractions to their lowest form by cancelling.

Examples A fraction can be changed to an equivalent fraction by:

CANCELLING $\frac{6}{9}\frac{(\div 3)}{(\div 3)} = \frac{2}{3}$ MULTIPLYING $\frac{3}{4}\frac{(\times 4)}{(\times 4)} = \frac{12}{16}$

A

Write the equivalent fractions shown by the shaded area in each pair of diagrams.

1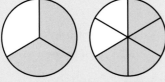

3

5

2

4

B

Continue these fraction chains for five further terms.

1 $\frac{1}{3} = \frac{2}{6} = \frac{3}{9}$

2 $\frac{3}{4} = \frac{6}{8} = \frac{9}{12}$

3 $\frac{7}{10} = \frac{14}{20} = \frac{21}{30}$

4 $\frac{5}{6} = \frac{10}{12} = \frac{15}{18}$

5 $\frac{11}{15} = \frac{22}{30} = \frac{33}{45}$

Copy and complete these equivalent fractions.

6 $\frac{1}{6} = \frac{4}{\square}$

7 $\frac{3}{8} = \frac{9}{\square}$

8 $\frac{5}{7} = \frac{25}{\square}$

9 $\frac{2}{3} = \frac{12}{\square}$

10 $\frac{7}{8} = \frac{35}{\square}$

11 $\frac{3}{4} = \frac{\square}{28}$

12 $\frac{2}{5} = \frac{\square}{25}$

13 $\frac{4}{9} = \frac{\square}{36}$

14 $\frac{7}{20} = \frac{\square}{100}$

15 $\frac{2}{7} = \frac{\square}{21}$

Cancel each fraction into its lowest form.

16 $\frac{12}{18}$

17 $\frac{6}{14}$

18 $\frac{52}{100}$

19 $\frac{36}{60}$

20 $\frac{28}{42}$

21 $\frac{44}{48}$

22 $\frac{27}{45}$

23 $\frac{14}{16}$

24 $\frac{450}{1000}$

25 $\frac{12}{32}$

C

Pick out the letters above the fractions equivalent to the fraction in the brackets.
Rearrange those letters to make a word using the clue.

1 ($\frac{1}{2}$, a fruit)

A	P	G	L	E	N	H	P	C	R
$\frac{7}{14}$	$\frac{6}{16}$	$\frac{8}{16}$	$\frac{4}{10}$	$\frac{2}{4}$	$\frac{3}{9}$	$\frac{12}{20}$	$\frac{5}{10}$	$\frac{25}{40}$	$\frac{9}{18}$

2 ($\frac{3}{4}$, a boy's name)

O	N	C	E	I	R	L	A	N	Y
$\frac{4}{6}$	$\frac{6}{8}$	$\frac{16}{20}$	$\frac{75}{100}$	$\frac{9}{15}$	$\frac{10}{16}$	$\frac{30}{40}$	$\frac{24}{30}$	$\frac{9}{12}$	$\frac{15}{20}$

3 ($\frac{2}{3}$, a European country)

A	N	G	E	T	S	L	E	D	W
$\frac{6}{10}$	$\frac{8}{12}$	$\frac{21}{30}$	$\frac{4}{6}$	$\frac{8}{15}$	$\frac{18}{27}$	$\frac{15}{24}$	$\frac{10}{15}$	$\frac{20}{30}$	$\frac{6}{9}$

4 ($\frac{5}{6}$, a girl's name)

A	P	A	L	T	I	R	N	O	D
$\frac{25}{30}$	$\frac{55}{60}$	$\frac{20}{26}$	$\frac{10}{12}$	$\frac{15}{24}$	$\frac{40}{48}$	$\frac{30}{42}$	$\frac{50}{60}$	$\frac{45}{63}$	$\frac{15}{18}$

5 Now make up a similar problem of your own.

I can compare and order fractions, decimals and percentages.

Examples

Arrange $\frac{1}{2}$, $\frac{3}{5}$, $\frac{8}{20}$ in ascending order.

Find a common denominator → 10

$\frac{1}{2} = \frac{5}{10}$ $\frac{3}{5} = \frac{6}{10}$ $\frac{8}{20} = \frac{4}{10}$

The correct order is $\frac{8}{20}$, $\frac{1}{2}$, $\frac{3}{5}$.

Arrange   0·53, $\frac{3}{5}$, 5%   in ascending order.

Change fraction and percentage to decimals.

$\frac{3}{5} = 0·6$ 5% = 0·05

The correct order is 5%,   0·53, $\frac{3}{5}$.

A

1 Which of the fractions in the box are:

   a) equal to one half

   b) less than one half

   c) greater than one half?

$\frac{2}{3}$	$\frac{4}{8}$	$\frac{2}{5}$	$\frac{7}{14}$	$\frac{5}{9}$
$\frac{3}{7}$	$\frac{7}{12}$	$\frac{15}{30}$	$\frac{9}{16}$	$\frac{5}{11}$

2 Copy the line and locate the numbers.

2	2·03	2·05
1·95	1·97	2·07

1·9   2·1

Write >, < or = in each box.

3 1% ☐ $\frac{1}{10}$

4 0·7 ☐ 70%

5 40% ☐ $\frac{1}{4}$

6 5% ☐ 0·05

7 $\frac{2}{5}$ ☐ 0·25

8 0·09 ☐ 9%

9 60% ☐ $\frac{6}{10}$

10 0·5 ☐ $\frac{1}{2}$

B

Arrange in ascending order.

1 $\frac{2}{3}$, $\frac{3}{4}$, $\frac{7}{12}$

2 $\frac{1}{3}$, $\frac{2}{5}$, $\frac{4}{15}$

3 $\frac{3}{4}$, $\frac{4}{5}$, $\frac{7}{10}$

4 $\frac{1}{3}$, $\frac{1}{6}$, $\frac{3}{12}$

Arrange in ascending order.

5 5·38, 3·85, 3·58, 5·8

6 2·49, 2·9, 2·94, 2·4

7 6·7, 6,37, 6·33, 6·337

8 5·202, 5·2, 5·22, 5·02

9 Copy the line and locate the numbers.

0·66	0·645	0·61
0·625	0·69	0·675

0·6   0·7

Write >, < or = in each box.

10 35% ☐ $\frac{3}{5}$ ☐ 0·5

11 75% ☐ $\frac{3}{4}$ ☐ 0·34

12 10% ☐ $\frac{1}{8}$ ☐ 0·8

13 40% ☐ $\frac{7}{10}$ ☐ 0·35

14 0·15 ☐ $\frac{1}{5}$ ☐ 0·2

15 0·4 ☐ $\frac{8}{10}$ ☐ 80%

16 0·19 ☐ $\frac{1}{9}$ ☐ 9%

17 0·56 ☐ $\frac{5}{6}$ ☐ 65%

C

Find the number which is halfway between:

1 2·1 and 2·6

2 0·43 and 0·5

3 1·03 and 0·98

4 26 and 29·3

5 $\frac{1}{4}$ and $\frac{7}{12}$

6 $\frac{4}{5}$ and $\frac{1}{2}$

7 $\frac{2}{3}$ and $\frac{1}{4}$

8 $\frac{5}{8}$ and 1

9 $4\frac{3}{5}$ and $4\frac{7}{10}$

10 $2\frac{1}{3}$ and $2\frac{1}{4}$

11 $1\frac{3}{4}$ and $1\frac{3}{5}$

12 $1\frac{5}{6}$ and $2\frac{3}{4}$

Write >, < or = in each box.

13 0·1 ☐ $\frac{1}{11}$ ☐ 11%

14 0·3 ☐ $\frac{1}{3}$ ☐ 33%

15 0·4 ☐ $\frac{1}{4}$ ☐ 44%

16 0·7 ☐ $\frac{4}{7}$ ☐ 47%

17 0·29 ☐ $\frac{2}{9}$ ☐ 20%

18 0·78 ☐ $\frac{7}{8}$ ☐ 87%

19 0·6 ☐ $\frac{7}{12}$ ☐ 70%

20 0·18 ☐ $\frac{1}{8}$ ☐ 8%

I can solve word problems involving several steps.

Example

A painting is 34 cm long and 25 cm wide.
Its frame will be 5 cm wide.
What area of the wall will the framed painting cover?

$34 + 5 + 5 = 44$
$25 + 5 + 5 = 35$
$44 \times 35 = 1540$
Area covered is 1540 cm²

A

1. How many hours are there in three weeks?

2. There were 143 skaters on an ice rink. During the next half hour 57 people started skating and 69 people stopped. How many skaters were there now on the rink?

3. One quarter of the 128 people on a school trip were adults. How many were children?

4. A greengrocer has seven boxes each containing 40 red apples. He also has five boxes of green apples. There are 400 apples altogether. How many green apples are there in each box?

5. 36 children were asked what was their favourite day of the week. One third chose Saturday and one quarter chose Sunday. How many chose a weekday?

B

1. Leslie runs 8·65 km three times each week. Nigel runs 6·8 km four times each week. How much further does Nigel run than Leslie in a week?

2. The perimeter of a rectangular field is 0·87 km. The longer sides are 236 m long. How long is each shorter side?

3. A computer normally costs £429. Its price is reduced by 20% in a sale. What is the sale price?

4. There are 280 children in a school. Three sevenths have brown hair and 35% have fair hair. How many children have hair of a different colour?

5. An ice cream van has seven packets each containing 65 chocolate flakes. During the day 163 are used. How many flakes are left?

C

1. The outside of a frame is 68 cm by 46 cm. The frame is 4·5 cm wide. What is the area of the painting inside the frame?

2. A theme park had 43 400 visitors in July. In August there were 15% more visitors. Altogether how many people visited the park in July and August?

3. In one year Colin earns £24 020. He pays no tax on the first £6500. Above this figure he pays 22% tax on all his income. How much tax should he pay?

4. A box containing 80 tea bags weighs 300 grams. The box weighs 24 grams. What is the weight of one tea bag?

5. There are 432 children in a school. Two ninths come by car. Five twelfths walk. How many children travel to school in other ways?

I can solve problems involving ratio and proportion.

Example
The ratio of white beads to black is 3:2.
There are 40 beads altogether. How many are white?
Answer   *24 white beads*

Method   3 + 2 = 5
          40 ÷ 5 = 8
          3 × 8 = 24

A

1

A necklace is made using this pattern of beads. How many red beads are there if there are:

a)   35 beads altogether

b)   35 yellow beads?

2 One can weighs 250 g. How many cans weigh 2 kg?

3 40 people are playing bowls. There are three people over 65 to every two people under 65. How many of the 40 bowlers are over 65?

4 Pink paint is made by mixing four times as much white paint as red. How much white paint is needed to make one litre of pink paint?

5 Class 5 has four boys to every three girls. There are 12 girls. How many boys are there?

6 A map has a scale of 1 cm to 2 km. On the map a road is 12 cm long. How long is the road?

B

1 Three in eight of the 240 cars produced in a factory are white. How many cars are not white?

2 The ratio of tents to caravans at a camp site is 3:4. There are 24 tents. How many caravans are there?

3 Orange paint is made by mixing yellow and red in a ratio of 5:3. How much yellow paint is needed to make two litres of orange?

4 Beef costs £8·00 for one kilogram. How much will 350 g cost?

5 A baker mixes brown flour and white flour in a ratio of 3:2. How much of each is needed for 4 kg of the mixed flour?

6 A map has a scale of 1 cm to 4 km. Two villages are 24 km apart. How far apart are they on the map?

C

1

A necklace is made using this pattern of beads. How many red beads are there if there are:

a)   30 green beads

b)   10 yellow beads

c)   40 beads altogether?

2 In one year the ratio of sunny days to cloudy days was 2:3. How many days were sunny?

3 Four in nine of the 360 dresses in a shop are sold. How many are left?

4 Cheese costs £6·40 per kilogram. How much can be bought for £1·60?

5 There are 180 people in a cinema. The ratio of children to adults is 7:5. How many children are in the audience?

6 A map has a scale of 1:100 000. What distance is shown by 5 cm on the map?

Work out

1. 1236×10
2. $4 \cdot 1 \times 10$
3. 240×100
4. 1597×100
5. 528×1000
6. 66×1000
7. $18\,750 \div 10$
8. $3 \cdot 0 \div 10$
9. $43\,700 \div 100$
10. $1\,250\,000 \div 100$
11. $85\,000 \div 1000$
12. $4\,630\,000 \div 1000$

Round to the nearest 10.

13. 136
15. 7245
14. 874
16. 1498

Round to the nearest 100.

17. 8648
19. 17 635
18. 26 971
20. 64 253

Round to the nearest 1000.

21. 16 379
23. 8542
22. 127 600
24. 59 837

Approximate by rounding to the nearest whole one.

25. $14 \cdot 6 + 8 \cdot 3$
26. $25 \cdot 5 - 17 \cdot 8$
27. $8 \cdot 6 \times 4 \cdot 1$
28. $53 \cdot 7 \div 5 \cdot 9$

Estimate the numbers shown by the arrows.

29. 50 ↓ ↓ 100
30. 0 ↓ ↓ 1
31. 25 ↓ ↓ 0
32. 50 ↓ ↓70
33. −20 ↓ ↓ 0
34. 0 ↓ ↓ 2

35. Copy and complete the table showing changes in temperature.

OLD	CHANGE	NEW
4°C	−19°C	
−7°C	+15°C	
−2°C		6°C
	−14°C	−3°C
−1°C	−8°C	
5°C		−11°C
	+9°C	4°C
−18°C	+13°C	
−13°C		3°C
	−17°C	12°C

Copy each sequence and write the next four terms.

36. 2·5 2·2 1·9 1·6
37. −20 −16 −12 −8
38. 79 68 57 46
39. 0·02 0·04 0·06 0·08
40. −14 −11 −8 −5
41. 10 20 40 70
42. 0·35 0·48 0·61 0·74
43. 100 81 64 49

Find three numbers that are multiples of both:

44. 6 and 7
46. 5 and 8
45. 4 and 13
47. 3 and 25.

Write down the first prime number after:

48. 8
52. 44
49. 14
53. 55
50. 20
54. 80
51. 32
55. 90.

Find all the prime factors of:

56. 27
59. 76
57. 66
60. 90
58. 45
61. 84.

Work out

62. $8^2 + 5^2$
65. 30^2
63. $9^2 - 7^2$
66. 11^2
64. $10^2 + 6^2$
67. 25^2

Copy and complete these equivalent fractions.

1. $\frac{3}{4} = \frac{\square}{20}$

2. $\frac{2}{5} = \frac{\square}{30}$

3. $\frac{7}{9} = \frac{\square}{18}$

4. $\frac{3}{10} = \frac{21}{\square}$

5. $\frac{5}{6} = \frac{15}{\square}$

6. $\frac{7}{8} = \frac{35}{\square}$

Cancel each fraction into its simplest form.

7. $\frac{33}{55}$

8. $\frac{80}{100}$

9. $\frac{22}{48}$

10. $\frac{18}{42}$

Arrange in ascending order.

11. $\frac{5}{8}, \frac{3}{4}, \frac{1}{2}, \frac{9}{16}$

12. $\frac{5}{12}, \frac{1}{3}, \frac{1}{2}, \frac{5}{9}$

Change to mixed numbers.

13. $\frac{14}{5}$

14. $\frac{27}{8}$

15. $\frac{57}{10}$

16. $\frac{14}{3}$

17. $\frac{319}{100}$

18. $\frac{60}{9}$

Change to improper fractions.

19. $8\frac{9}{10}$

20. $3\frac{5}{6}$

21. $6\frac{7}{11}$

22. $2\frac{17}{25}$

Write the fraction shaded in its simplest form.

23.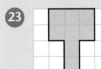

24.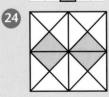

Write as decimals.

25. $4\frac{32}{100}$

26. $1\frac{723}{1000}$

27. $\frac{86}{1000}$

28. $2\frac{9}{100}$

Write as mixed numbers.

29. 5·35

30. 23·04

31. 6·127

32. 2·008

Write the value of the underlined digit.

33. 7·2$\underline{5}$

34. 0·80$\underline{1}$

35. 1$\underline{7}$·08

36. 5·7$\underline{3}$6

37. 2·47$\underline{9}$

38. 48·$\underline{6}$2

39. 0·10$\underline{5}$

40. 12·9$\underline{4}$

41. Copy the line and locate the numbers.

1·05 1·08 1·025 1·065

1·0   1·1

42. Write the number shown by each arrow.

0·6   0·7

Round to the nearest:

whole one

43. 3·74

44. 4·29

45. 29·81

46. 106·52

tenth

47. 4·61

48. 29·38

49. 3·45

50. 37·83

51. Write in ascending order.

7·58, 0·78, 0·708, 7·08

52. Copy and complete the table.

Fraction	Decimal	%
$\frac{1}{10}$	0·1	10%
$\frac{37}{100}$		
$\frac{3}{4}$		
	0·72	
	0·3	
	0·09	
		50%
		23%
		7%

Find

53. $\frac{3}{8}$ of 40

54. $\frac{4}{5}$ of 60

55. $\frac{23}{100}$ of 3 m

56. $\frac{375}{1000}$ of 1 m

57. 10% of 58

58. 30% of 240

59. 20% of £14·00

60. 5% of £6·20

61. Lenny has 3 green marbles to every 4 red marbles. If he has 20 red marbles, how many green marbles does he have?

62. 8000 people visited a castle. 70% were adults. How many were children?

CALCULATIONS REVIEW

Copy and complete.

1. $305 + 298 = \square$
2. $4\cdot8 + 3\cdot1 = \square$
3. $5\cdot7 + \square = 9\cdot5$
4. $3\cdot64 + \square = 4$
5. $\square + 6700 = 14\,300$
6. $\square + 0\cdot37 = 0\cdot87$

7. $4003 - 1986 = \square$
8. $8\cdot6 - 1\cdot9 = \square$
9. $4300 - \square = 1900$
10. $7\cdot1 - \square = 2\cdot8$
11. $\square - 0\cdot16 = 0\cdot6$
12. $\square - 5800 = 3700$

Work out

13. $3249 + 1563$
14. $4385 + 3948$
15. $5167 + 1856$
16. $6478 + 2757$
17. $4753 - 1278$
18. $7480 - 2916$
19. $9619 - 5834$
20. $6250 - 5791$

Set out correctly and find the totals.

21. $1\cdot25 + 14\cdot6$
22. $0\cdot309 + 8\cdot4$
23. $4\cdot31 + 17\cdot2 + 0\cdot695$
24. $25\cdot91 + 0\cdot8 + 1\cdot357$

Set out correctly and find the differences.

25. 7186 and 15 470
26. 729 and 42 031
27. $5\cdot31 - 1\cdot9$
28. $3\cdot2 - 1\cdot85$

Copy and complete.

29. $7 \times 0\cdot6 = \square$
30. $15 \times 99 = \square$
31. $8 \times \square = 4\cdot0$
32. $1\cdot3 \times \square = 1\cdot3$
33. $\square \times 100 = 30$
34. $\square \times 7 = 4\cdot9$

35. $27 \div 10 = \square$
36. $0\cdot3 \div 3 = \square$
37. $12 \div \square = 0\cdot6$
38. $300 \div \square = 60$
39. $\square \div 6 = 1\cdot4$
40. $\square \div 100 = 3\cdot7$

Copy and complete.

41. 1576×4
42. 2938×7
43. 4629×6
44. 3574×8

Copy and complete.

45. $23\overline{)713}$
46. $14\overline{)314}$
47. $5\overline{)83\cdot5}$
48. $9\overline{)312\cdot3}$

Copy and complete.

49. 325×19
50. 276×47

Work out

51. $2\cdot38 \times 3$
52. $0\cdot56 \times 6$
53. $4\cdot72 \times 7$
54. $3\cdot95 \times 9$

Work out and give the remainder as a fraction.

55. $86 \div 6$
56. $158 \div 9$
57. $389 \div 100$
58. $160 \div 7$

Work out and give the remainder as a decimal.

59. $126 \div 10$
60. $74 \div 4$
61. $67 \div 5$
62. $190 \div 8$

63. Ai Ping has £3159 in her bank account. She withdraws £1374. How much is left in the account?

64. How many hours are there in December?

65. A box holds 16 tins. How many boxes can be filled from 360 tins? How many tins are left over?

66. There are 28 nails in each bag. How many nails are there in 35 bags?

Copy and complete.

1. 1·738 km = ☐ m

2. 27 m = ☐ km

3. 9 cm = ☐ m

4. 1·3 m = ☐ cm

5. 0·146 m = ☐ mm

6. 8 mm = ☐ cm

7. 0·7 m = ☐ cm

8. 395 m = ☐ km

9. 2·8 kg = ☐ g

10. 1·55 kg = ☐ g

11. 368 g = ☐ kg

12. 4970 g = ☐ kg

13. 0·6 litres = ☐ ml

14. 1·9 litres = ☐ ml

15. 50 ml = ☐ litres

16. 3820 ml = ☐ litres

Work out the measurement shown by each arrow.

17.

18.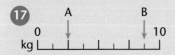

19. litres 20. kg

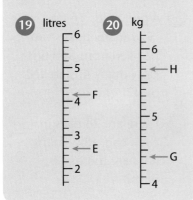

21. 70 ml of wine is poured equally into 5 glasses. How much wine does each glass contain?

22. A ribbon is 1·8 m long. 137 mm is cut off. How long is the ribbon which is left?

23. A train travels at 40 metres per second. How many kilometres will it travel in one hour?

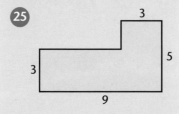

24. The 40 tins of tuna in a box weigh 10 kg. What does each tin weigh in grams?

For each shape work out:

a) the area

b) the perimeter.

(All lengths are in cm.)

25.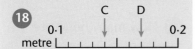

26.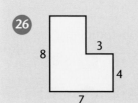

Copy and complete.

27. 85 years = ☐ decades

28. 91 days = ☐ weeks

29. 132 hours = ☐ days

30. 540 secs = ☐ mins

31. 1 day = ☐ minutes

32. 3 decades = ☐ months

33. 2 weeks = ☐ hours

34. 2 hours = ☐ seconds

35. What will be the date four weeks after:
    a) October 15th
    b) April 23rd
    c) February 8th 2016
    d) December 25th?

36. Turkey must be cooked for 40 minutes for every kilogram. Copy and complete the table.

WEIGHT	START	FINISH
5 kg	15:45	
6·5 kg	08:30	
9·5 kg	06:25	
7·5 kg	12:50	

37. The time in Tokyo is 9 hours ahead of the time in London. What is the time in Tokyo if the time in London is:
    a) 08:00
    b) 19:00?

Write the names of each of these 2-D shapes.

1   **5**

2   **6**

3   **7**

4   **8**

9 Which of the above shapes have:

a) parallel lines

b) perpendicular lines

c) equal opposite angles

d) equal adjacent angles?

Use squared paper. Copy the shape and the mirror line and sketch the reflection.

10   **11**

12

For each 3-D shape.

a) write its name

b) describe its flat faces.

13   **14**

15

16 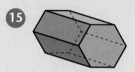   **17**

18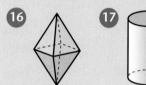

19   **20**

How many cubes are needed to build each shape?

21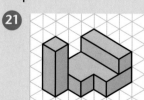

22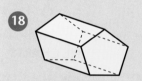

23 Copy the grid and the triangle.

Translate the triangle:

a) Right 2, Up 2

b) Left 1, Down 2.

Give the co-ordinates of the two new positions.

24 Copy the grid above. Plot these points and join them up in this order.
(3, 4) (3, 6) (4, 6) (4, 5) (6, 5) (6, 4) (3, 4)
Rotate the shape about (3, 4):

a) 90° clockwise

b) 180°.

Use a protractor. Draw these angles.

25 76°   **27** 18°

26 143°   **28** 102°

Calculate the missing angles.

29   **30**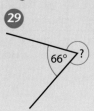

29 66° ?

30 ? / 70° 80°

INTERPRETING DATA

For questions **1** to **3** find:

a) the range

c) the median

b) the mode

d) the mean.

1 The numbers of paintings completed each day by an artist.

```
3  1  0  2
3  4  0  1
2  4  1  5
0  1  3
```

2 The daily maximum temperatures recorded in one week in March.

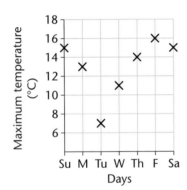

3 The numbers of shoes sold by a shop in each hour of trading.

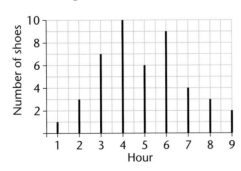

BAR CHARTS WITH GROUPED DATA

4 This bar chart shows the marks achieved by children in a test.

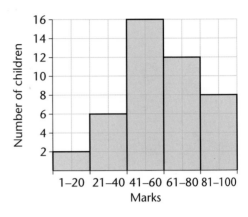

a) How many children scored between 41 and 60 marks?

b) How many children scored over 60 marks

c) How many children took the test?

PIE CHARTS

5 This pie chart shows how 72 people travelled to the same hotel.
Write down how many people travelled by:

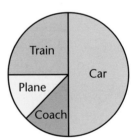

a) train

b) car

c) plane.

6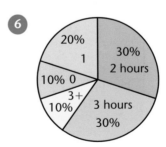

This pie chart shows the number of hours in one evening spent watching television by 40 children.

Work out the number of children in each sector.